THE LIFE OF JOHN OWEN

Andrew Thompson

GLH Publishing
Louisville, KY

Sourced from *The Works of John Owen*, Vol. I.
  T&T Clark, Edinburgh, 1862.

Republished by GLH Publishing, 2020.

ISBN:
  Paperback 978-1-64863-016-3
  Epub 978-1-64863-017-0

Contents

I. His Student-Life 1

II. His Pastorate 16

III. His Vice-Chancellorship 38

IV. His Retirement and Last Days 68

Appendix to the Life of Dr Owen 131

    I. Epitaph inscribed on the Monument of Dr Owen in Bunhill-fields 131

    II. Some Letters 134

    III. His Works 146

I. His Student-Life

It is matter of just regret and complaint that no elaborate contemporary memoir of this great Puritan was ever written. Twenty years after his death, Cotton Mather, in his *"Magnalia Americana Christi,"* declared "that the church of God was wronged, in that the life of the great John Owen was not written;" and it was only when twenty years more had elapsed that a life of Owen at length appeared, from the pen of Mr Asty, a respectable Independent minister in London; which, though written under the eye of Sir John Hartopp, a particular friend of Owen, and for many years a member of his church, is chargeable with numerous inaccuracies, and so scanty withal, as "not to contain so many pages as Owen has written books."[1] In addition to this, an equally brief anonymous memoir has fallen into our hands, professing to have been written by one who "had the honour to know this eminent person well, and to hear him frequently; though he must confess that he had not then years and experience enough to conceive a suitable idea of the Doctor's great worth." But the student who should wish to search for voluminous contemporary records and early reminiscences of Owen, will look in vain for such full and accurate memorials as Dr Edmund Calamy has given us of Howe; for such an inexhaustible storehouse of incident, and almost redundance of mental portraiture, as Richard Baxter has given us of himself. The sources from which the modern biographer must draw his notices of Owen, besides those already named, are to some extent the representations of adversaries, who could not be silent

---

1 Orme's Memoirs of Owen, p. 2.

on so great a name, or withhold reluctant praise; the not infrequent allusions to Owen in the lives of his contemporaries; the statements of general history and biography, — such as are to be found in the page of Neal, Calamy, Middleton, Palmer, and others; and, perhaps the most valuable and interesting of all, the many unconscious touches of autobiography which may be found in his prefaces to his various works. Of all of these Mr Orme has made excellent use in his Life of Owen; which is a remarkable specimen of untiring research, solid judgment and ability in the disposal of his materials, and, making some allowance for honest bias, of biographical fidelity: and from all of these, and especially from Mr Orme himself, we shall gather the details of our biographical sketch and estimate of Owen.

The genealogy of the subject of our memoir leads us back to a family of high rank and reputation in Wales, whose remoter links connect it with the five regal tribes. In the reigns of Henry VIII., Edward VI., and Queen Mary, we meet with the name of Lewis Owen as Vice-chamberlain and Baron of the Exchequer in North Wales, and High Sheriff of the county of Merioneth; as honoured by correspondence with those monarchs in reference to the affairs of Wales and as going forth on a commission to clear the country of those felons and outlaws who had sought refuge in great numbers among its mountains, during the turbulence and relaxed authority that had arisen from the long wars between the houses of York and Lancaster. At a later period this honoured ancestor fell a sacrifice to his fidelity as a magistrate; for, on his return from the assizes in Montgomeryshire, he fell into the hands of a band of outlaws, who had taken a vow of revenge against him on account of the capture of their companions, and, deserted by all but one faithful friend, was murdered by them in the woods of Monthrey.[2]

Humphrey Owen, a branch of this same family, married Susan, a granddaughter of Lewis Owen; and to him there were born in succession fifteen sons, the youngest of whom was Hen-

---

2 Asty's Memoir, p. ii. Anonymous Memoir, p. v.

ry Owen. Henry was dedicated by his parents to office in the church, and having received an education, in language, philosophy, and divinity, at Oxford, in the course of time became vicar of Stadham, in Oxfordshire. Here he proved himself so "painful a labourer in the vineyard of the Lord," and so uncompromising an advocate for reformation in the church, as to receive testimony to his fidelity in the jealousy and displeasure of the dominant ecclesiastical powers, and to be branded with the name of "Puritan." To this worthy vicar there was born, at Stadham, in the year 1616, a second son, JOHN OWEN, the subject of this memoir, who was destined to shed a new renown on their ancient house, and to eclipse, by the more substantial glory of his virtues, learning, and genius, the dim lustre of their regal lineage.[3]

Little is known regarding the childhood of Owen; and no records whatever have descended to tell us of the mother to whom was committed the training of his most susceptible years, and who was to be the Monnica to this future Augustine. There is reason to think that he received the elements of a common education from the good vicar himself, under the domestic roof at Stadham; while, after a few years of home education, he was transferred to a private academy at Oxford, where he entered on his classical studies under the superintendence of Edward Sylvester, a tutor of eminence, several of whose pupils rose to the highest distinction, and even won for themselves at no distant date an undying fame. A comparison of dates makes it unlikely that the two were playmates; but it is interesting to notice, that the same quiet institution, in the parish of All-Saints, which now received within its walls the future great theologian of the Puritans, was also the place in which was initiated into the Greek and Roman tongues the immortal Chillingworth, — of whose great work, "The Religion of Protestants," it is not too much to say, that it is sufficient to shed honour, not on a

---

3 Ibid.

university merely, but on an age.[4] One fact will suffice to show the energy with which the young pupil applied himself to his studies, as well as the unusually early development of his faculties, that, at the age of twelve, he was found to have outgrown the instructions of Sylvester and to be ripe for the university. He was, accordingly, entered a student at Queen's College at this age, which, in the case of most youths, would have been most injudiciously premature, and, even at this period, must have seemed strangely early; for, in looking into the lives of some of the most eminent of his contemporaries, we meet with no instance of similar precocity. Bishop Hall, for example, enrolled himself at Cambridge at fifteen,[5] while his great Puritan contemporary, John Howe, did not enter Oxford until he had reached the riper age of seventeen.[6]

Few men of great eminence appear to have occupied the chairs of the university at this period; but Owen was fortunate enough to have his studies in mathematics and philosophy superintended by a tutor of solid attainments and subsequent high distinction, — Thomas Barlow, then a fellow of Queen's College, afterwards its provost, and who, in course of time, was elevated to the see of Lincoln.[7] The boy-student devoted himself to the various branches of learning with an intensity that

---

4   Wood's *Athenæ Oxoniensis*, p. 97. Orme, p. 7.

5   Hamilton's Memoir of Bishop Hall, p. viii.

6   Urwick's Life of Howe, p. vi.

7   We have additional authority for many of the above facts in one of the *larger* epitaphs on Owen by his friend the Rev. T. Gilbert of Oxford; some lines of which we subjoin:—

"*Literis natus, literis innutritus, totusque deditus;*
Donec animata plane evasit bibliotheca:
Authoribus classicis, qua Græcis, qua Latinis,
Sub Edv. Sylvestro, scholæ privitæ Oxonii moderatore
Operam navavit satis felicem:
Feliciorem adhuc studiis philosophicis,
Magno sub Barlovi, coll. reginalis, id tempus, socio."

would have unhinged most minds, and broken in pieces any bodily constitution except the most robust. For several years of his university curriculum he allowed himself only four hours of the night for sleep, though he had the wisdom so far to counteract the injurious influence of sedentary habits and excessive mental toil, by having recourse to bodily recreation in some of its most robust and even violent forms. Leaping, throwing the bar, bell-ringing, and similar amusements, occasionally allured him from his books; and it may perhaps surprise some, who conceive of the men of that age as unsocial and unfriendly to all the lighter graces and accomplishments, to learn that Owen received lessons in music from Dr Thomas Wilson, a celebrated performer on the flute, and the favourite preceptor in the same elegant and delightful art of Charles I. It may perhaps have been from grateful recollections of these youthful and fascinating exercises, in which the student had been accustomed to unbend from too protracted and severe studies, that Owen at a future period, when elevated to the vice-chancellorship of Oxford, appointed his early tutor professor of music in the university.[8]

Still, the hours which are taken from needful rest are not redeemed, but borrowed, and must be paid back with double interest in future life; and Owen, when he began to feel his iron frame required to pay the penalty of his youthful enthusiasm, was accustomed to declare that he would willingly part with all the learning he had accumulated by such means, if he might but recover the health which he had lost in the gaining of it. And he was wont to confess with a far profounder sorrow, not unmixed with shame, that no holy oil at this time fed his midnight lamp; but that the great motive which had borne him up, during those days and nights of consuming toil, was an ambition to rise to distinction and power in the church. We can well believe that the severity of this self-condemnation would, by a judge more tender than himself, have so far been mitigated by the knowledge of another motive, which must have had considerable in-

---

8   Asty, p. iii. Orme, p. 9.

fluence upon his mind, arising from the fact that his father had been unable to render him any adequate pecuniary assistance, and that he had hitherto been indebted for his support to the liberality of an uncle in Wales. But still, when more amiable motives have been allowed their full force, a mere earthly ambition must be acknowledged to have been the mainspring of all his past efforts; and we cannot doubt that, when he returned to the university at a future period, these condemnatory reminiscences arose strongly in his mind, and that, like Philip Henry in similar circumstances, while thanking God that his course had been unstained by vices, he could insert in his book, "A tear dropped over my university sins."[9]

And here let us pause for a moment, to look at the circumstances of another student, who was destined at a future day to shine with Owen in the same bright constellation. While Owen was walking amid the majestic structures and academic shades of Oxford, or bending over the midnight page, Richard Baxter might have been seen amid the enchanting scenery of Ludlow Castle, or, later still, in the small village of Wroxeter, with little help or guidance from man, but, under the promptings of an indomitable will, and with an omnivorous appetite for knowledge, allowing no difficulties or discouragements to damp the ardour of his pursuits. Without the advantage of the systematic training of a university, or the command of the rich stores of its libraries, this was almost compensated to his athletic soul by the more discursive and varied range which both his tastes and his necessities thus gave to his studies. In the writings of Thomas Aquinas, Anselm, and Duns Scotus, which to most minds would have been dry and barren as the sands of the desert, his acute intellect found high exercise and real delight, and rejoiced in whetting and exercising on them its dialectic powers, until he could rival in subtle and shadowy distinctions those ghostly schoolmen. Two years the senior of Owen, he was also "in Christ" before him; and while the Oxford student was still

---

9   Bogue and Bennet's History of Dissenters, ii. 211, 226.

I. His Student-Life

feeding the fires of an earth-born ambition, Baxter had learned from Sibbs' Bruised Reed, and from his Bible, the art of holy meditation; and, even in the later years of his student-life, might have been seen at that hour when it was too dark to read and too early to light his lamp, devoting its sacred moments to thinking of heaven and anticipations of the "saints' everlasting rest."[10] But the same grace was soon to descend upon the soul of Owen, and, cooperating with providential occurrences, to withdraw him forever from the poor daydreams of a mere earthly ambition. While he was measuring out for himself a course which, if successful, would probably have made him a secular churchman, and even an intolerant persecutor, Christ had said of him, "I will show him how great things he must suffer for my name's sake." Let us now trace the influences and events which brought about in the mind and outward circumstances of Owen this mighty change.

We have no minute information regarding the means by which his mind was first turned with serious personal interest to the supreme subject of religion. Perhaps the dormant seeds of early instruction that had been lodged in his mind under the roof of the humble vicarage now began to live; perhaps some of those truths which he was storing in his mind as matter of mere intellectual furniture and accomplishment had unexpectedly reached his heart; or the earnest struggles on religious questions that were beginning to agitate the kingdom had, in some measure, arrested the sympathy of the young recluse; or thoughts of a more serious kind than he had yet entertained had arisen in his mind, he knew not how, like invisible and life-awakening spring-breezes; or all these things combined may have been employed as influences in bringing him at length to "seek first the kingdom of God, and his righteousness." At all events, we have Owen's own testimony to the fact, that in the later years of his university life, the Divine Spirit began to work in his soul a new class of thoughts and emotions; and though it was not until a

---

10 Jenkyn's Essay on the Life of Baxter, pp. iii.–v.

later period that he entered upon the full peace and holy liberty of the kingdom of God, he was brought even then to submit his life to the supreme control of religious principle, and to ask, "What wilt thou have me to do?"

While his mind was undergoing this great change, events were occurring in the government of the university which were fitted to put his religious principle to the test, and to try it, as it were, by fire. William Laud having, by a succession of rapid advancements, been raised to the chancellorship of Oxford, hastened to introduce into it those Romish innovations which, as the privy councillor and principal adviser of Charles, and the intimate associate of Strafford, he had already done much to infuse into the general ecclesiastical policy of the nation. The naturally arrogant and domineering spirit of this narrow-minded ecclesiastic, whom even Clarendon describes as "rough of temper, impatient of contradiction, and arbitrary,"[11] had far more to do with those oppressive measures which marked his fatal ecclesiastical supremacy, than those mistaken views of the rights of conscience which at this period dragged so many better and more amiable men into the ranks of persecutors. Accordingly, we find him requiring the adoption, by the university, of many of those rites and ceremonials which savoured the most strongly of Popish superstitions, and in some instances were identical with them, and which the Reformers of England had soonest renounced and most severely condemned; the penalty of resistance to this demand being nothing less than expulsion from the university.

This bold innovation at once dragged Owen from the privacy of his student-life into all the stern struggles of a public career. And his mind, delivered by the fear of God from every other fear, was not slow in resolving on resistance to the bigoted prelate's intolerant statutes. Many of the rites which Laud imposed were such as he in conscience believed to be divinely forbidden; and even things which, if left unimposed, might have

---

11 Heylin's Life of Laud, p. 252.

I. His Student-Life

been borne with as matters of indifference, when authoritatively enjoined as of equal obligation with divine appointment, he felt ought to be resisted as an invasion of the divine prerogative and the rights of conscience, — "a teaching for doctrines of the commandments of men." This was the ground that had been occupied by the Puritans from the days of Elizabeth, when Ridley and Latimer had "played the man in the fire;" and though we have no record of Owen's mental exercise at this period, yet, with the course that was actually taken by him before us, we cannot doubt that he now unconsciously felt his way to this first Puritan standing-point, and that the following passage, written by him long afterwards, expressed the principles which animated his mind and decided his movements: —

> "They [believers] will receive nothing, practise nothing, own nothing in His worship, but what is of His appointment. They know that from the foundation of the world he never did allow, nor ever will, that in any thing the will of the creatures should be the measure of his honour, or the principle of His worship, either as to matter or manner. It was a witty and true sense that one gave of the Second Commandment, 'Non imago, non simulachrum prohibetur, sed, non facies tibi;' — it is a making to ourselves, an inventing, a finding out ways of worship, or means of honouring God, not by him appointed, that is so severely forbidden. Believers know what entertainment all will-worship finds with God. 'Who has required this at your hand?' and, 'In vain do ye worship me, teaching for doctrines the traditions of men,' is the best it meets with. I shall take leave to say what is upon my heart, and what (the Lord assisting) I shall willing endeavour to make good against all the world, — namely, that that principle, that the church has power to institute and appoint any thing or ceremony belonging to the worship of God, either as to matter or to manner, beyond the orderly observance of such circumstances as necessarily attend such ordinances as Christ himself has instituted, lies at the bottom of all the horrible superstition and idolatry, of all

the confusion, blood, persecution, and wars, that have for so long a season spread themselves over the face of the Christian world; and that it is the design of a great part of the Book of the Revelation to make a discovery of this truth.

"And I doubt not but that the great controversy which God has had with this nation for so many years, and which he has pursued with so much anger and indignation, was upon this account, that, contrary to the glorious light of the Gospel, which shone among us, the wills and fancies of men, under the name of order, decency, and authority of the church (a chimera that none knew what it was, not wherein the power did consist, nor in whom reside), were imposed on men in the ways and worship of God. Neither was all that pretence of glory, beauty, comeliness, and conformity, that then was pleaded, any thing more or less than what God does so describe in the Church of Israel, Ezek. xvi. 25, and forwards. Hence was the Spirit of God in prayer derided, — hence was the powerful preaching of the gospel despised, — hence was the Sabbath-day decried, — hence was holiness stigmatized and persecuted. To what ends that Jesus Christ might be deposed from the sole power of lawmaking in his church, — that the true husband might be thrust aside, and adulterers of his spouse embraced, — that taskmasters might be appointed in and over his house, which he never *gave to his church,* Eph. iv. 11, — that a ceremonious, pompous, outward show-worship, drawn from Pagan, Judaical, and Antichristian observances, might be introduced; of all which there is not one word, tittle, or iota in the whole book of God. This, then, they who hold communion with Christ are careful of, — they will admit nothing, practise nothing, in the worship of God, private or public, but what they have his warrant for. Unless it comes in his name, with 'Thus saith the Lord Jesus,' they will not hear an angel from heaven."[12]

While the well-informed conscience of Owen thus distinctly forbade conformity, every consideration of seeming worldly

---

12 Owen on Communion with God, pp. 309, 310, fol. ed.

I. His Student-Life

interest strongly pleaded for pliant acquiescence in the statutes of Laud. To abandon Oxford, was to dash from him at once all those fair prospects which had hitherto shone before him in his career as a student, — to shut against himself the door, not only of honourable preferment, but, as it probably at this time appeared to his mind, of Christian usefulness, — to incur the inevitable displeasure of that prelate, whose keen and sleepless efforts to search out all who were opposed to his policy had already subjected every corner of the realm to a vigilant and minute inspection, and whose cruel and malignant spirit was already finding desolating scope in the unconstitutional measures and atrocities of the Star Chamber and the High Commission. And even though these latter perils might seem to be remote as yet from his head, yet could he not be blind to the fact, that, by such a step, he might incur the implacable displeasure of his Royalist uncle in Wales, who had hitherto supplied him with the principal means of support at Oxford, and expressed his intention, in case of continued satisfaction with his conduct, of making him heir to his estates. Yet all these probable consequences of non-compliance Owen was willing to incur, rather than violate his sense of duty, "esteeming the reproach of Christ greater riches than all the treasures of Egypt;" and, at the age of twenty-one, might have been seen leaving behind him all the daydreams and cherished associations of more than ten youthful years, and passing through the gates of Oxford self-exiled for conscience' sake. God was now educating him in a higher school than that of Oxford, and subjecting him to that fiery discipline by which he tempers and fashions his most chosen instruments. But "there is no man that has left house, or parents, or brethren, or wife, or children, for the kingdom of God's sake, who shall not receive manifold more in this present time, and in the world to come life everlasting." Ten years afterwards the banished student, who had thus nobly followed the light of conscience, lead where it might, was to be seen returning through those very gates to receive its highest honours, — to have intrusted to him the administration of its laws, and almost to occupy the very seat of power from which Laud had, in the interval, been ignominiously hurled.

Owen had "commenced master of arts" in his nineteenth year, and not long before leaving Oxford, had been admitted to orders by Bishop Bancroft. He now found a home unexpectedly opened to him in the house of Sir Philip Dormer of Ascot, who invited him to become chaplain to his family, and tutor to his eldest son; "in both which respects," says one of the oldest notices of Owen, "he acquitted himself with great satisfaction to Sir Robert and his family."[13] After some time, he accepted the situation of chaplain in the family of Lord Lovelace of Hurly, in Berkshire, where he appears to have enjoyed much kindness, and to have been duly appreciated.[14] But meanwhile the rent between Charles and his Parliament was widening apace. His frequent invasion of the constitutional rights of the other estates of the realm, his attempts to rule without a Parliament and to raise money by illegal means, his systematic violation of his most solemn pledges, his connivance at the innovating superstitions of Laud, and wanton violation of religious liberty, at length roused an impatient kingdom to resistance, drove the Parliament to the last resort of arms, and shook the land with the discord of civil war.[15] At such a crisis it is impossible for any man to remain neutral, and it found Owen and his patron of opposite sentiments. Lord Lovelace took up arms on the side of Charles, and of royal prerogative; all the convictions and sympathies of Owen were naturally with the army of the Parliament, and the cause of public liberty. Two consequences immediately followed from this to Owen, — his leaving the family of Lord Lovelace, and the complete estrangement of his

---

13 Anon. Mem., p. ix.

14 Wood's Athen. Oxen., p. 97.

15 Vaughen's Memorials of the Stuart Dynasty, I., ch. vii.–xi.

I. His Student-Life

Royalist uncle in Wales, who now finally disinherited him, and bestowed his estates and wealth upon another.

Leaving Berkshire, Owen now removed to London, and took up his residence in Charter-House Yard. Here he continued to suffer from that mental depression which had begun with his earliest religious anxieties at Oxford; and which, though partially relieved at intervals, had never yet been completely removed. Some influence is no doubt to be ascribed to the discouraging outward circumstances in which his uncle's conduct had placed him, in deepening the gloom of those shadows which now cast themselves across his spirit; but the chief spring of his distress lay deeper, — in his perplexities and anxieties about his state with God. For years he had been under the power of religious principle, but he had not yet been borne into the region of settled peace; and at times the terrors of the Lord seemed still to compass him about. We have no means of ascertaining with certainty what were the causes of these dreadful conflicts in Owen's mind; whether an overwhelming sense of the holiness and rectitude of God; or perverse speculations about the secret purposes of God, when he should have been reposing in his revealed truths and all embracing calls; or a self-righteous introversion of his thoughts upon himself, when he should have been standing in the full sun-light of the cross; or more mysterious deeps of anguish than any of these; — but we are disposed to think that his noble treatise on the "Forgiveness of Sin," written many years afterwards, is in a great degree the effect as well as the record of what he suffered now. Nothing is more certain than that some of the most precious treasures in our religious literature have thus come forth from the seven-times-heated furnace of mental suffering. The wondrous colloquies of Luther, in his "Introduction to the Galatians," reflect the conflicts of his own mighty spirit with unbelief; the "Pilgrim's Progress" is in no small degree the mental autobiography of Bunyan; and there is strong internal evidence that Owen's "Exposition of the 130th Psalm" — which is as full of Christian experience as of rich theology, and contains some of the noblest passages that Owen ever penned — is to a great extent the unconscious transcript of his present wanderings, and perplexities, and final deliverances.

But the time had come when the burden was to fall from Owen's shoulders; and few things in his life are more truly interesting than the means by which it was unloosed. Dr Edmund Calamy was at this time minister in Aldermanbury Chapel, and attracted multitudes by his manly eloquence. Owen had gone one Sabbath morning to hear the celebrated Presbyterian preacher, and was much disappointed when he saw an unknown stranger from the country enter the pulpit. His companion suggested that they should leave the chapel, and hasten to the peace of worship of another celebrated preacher; but Owen's strength being already exhausted, he determined to remain. After a prayer of simple earnestness, the text was announced in these words of Matt. viii. 26, "Why are ye fearful, O ye of little faith?" Immediately it arrested the thoughts of Owen as appropriate to his present state of mind, and he breathed an inward prayer that God would be pleased by that minister to speak to his condition. The prayer was heard, for the preacher stated and answered the very doubts that had long perplexed Owen's mind; and by the time that the discourse was ended, had succeeded in leading him forth into the sunshine of a settled peace. The most diligent efforts were used by Owen to discover the name of the preacher who had thus been to him "as an angel of God," but without success.[16]

There is a marked divine selection visible in the humble instrument that was thus employed to bring peace to Owen's mind. We trace in it the same wisdom that sent a humble Ananias to remove the scales from the eyes of Saul, and made the poor tent-maker and his wife the instructors of the eloquent Apollos. And can we doubt that when the fame of Owen's learning and intellectual power had spread far and wide, so that even foreign divines are said to have studied our language in order

---

16   Asty, p. v. Anon. Mem., p. x.

I. His Student-Life

that they might read his works the recollection of the mode of his own spiritual deliverance would repress all self-dependence and elation, and make him feel that the highest form of success in preaching was in no respect the monopoly of high intellectual gifts; but that in every instance it was, "not by might, nor by power, but by my Spirit, saith the Lord?"

II. His Pastorate

The mind of Owen, now effectually relieved from the burden of spiritual distress, soon recovered its elasticity and vigour; and in March 1642 he gave to the world his first literary production, — "The Display of Arminianism." In all likelihood he had been silently labouring at this work while in the families of Sir Philip Dormer and Lord Lovelace; more especially as his mental distress may have had some connection with a misunderstanding of certain of those points of which the Arminian controversy touches, and have led to their more full examination. But we may discover the principal occasion of the work in the ecclesiastical policy of the period, and in the strain of doctrinal sentiment which that policy had long aimed to foster and to propagate. Laud and his party had shown themselves as zealous for the peculiar dogmas of Arminianism, as for Romish rites and vestment and for passive obedience; and the dogmas had been received into royal favour because of their association with the advocacy of superstitious ceremonies and the defence of despotic rule. Arminianism having thus been constituted the exclusive way to preferment, had become the fashionable creed; and a current of doctrine had flowed into the church which was rapidly changing the character of its ministration, and bearing it away from those safe moorings at which its own articles and its Reformers had fixed it.

A remark by Owen, in his address to the reader, correctly describes the Laudean policy: "Had a poor Puritan offended against half so many *canons* as they opposed *articles*, he had forfeited his livelihood, if not endangered his life." And in another passage he explains the progress of Arminianism in England: "The chief cause I take to be that which Æneas Sylvius gave, why more maintained the pope to be above the council than the council above the pope; — because the popes gave archbishoprics and bishoprics, &c, but the councils sued '*in forma pauperis*,' and therefore could scarce get an advocate to plead their cause. The fates of our church having of late devolved the government of it on men tainted with this poison, Arminianism became backed with the powerful arguments of praise and preferment, and quickly beat poor naked Truth into a corner."

Owen's "Display" is a barrier raised against prevailing opinions. Each chapter contains a statement of the Arminian doctrine on the point discussed, with Owen's answer; while at the end of each chapter the Arminian doctrine is more briefly stated, in the language of some Arminian writer, and confronted in opposite columns by passages of Scripture. Undoubtedly there are some things charged upon the Arminianism of those times which belong rather to the family of Pelagian errors, and which the pious Arminian of our own day would at all events repudiate. Nor is it to be denied that the work is not free, in some parts, of the fault which clings to so much theological controversy, — that of making individuals responsible, not only for the opinions they avow, but for all the consequences that you may deduce from them; yet, withal, it is rich in matter which must have staggered the courtly theologians of the age, — is hung all round with massive Calvinistic armour; and, though written in a more scholastic form than most of Owen's subsequent works, gives indication of that spirit which was so characteristic of the Puritans, and pre-eminently of Owen, and which gave such a depth to their piety, — the spirit which connected all events with God, and bent with lowly and awe-struck feeling before the divine sovereignty.

Owen dedicated his work to "The Lords and Gentlemen of the committee for Religion;" who appointed it to be printed by the Committee of the House of Commons for regulating the printing and publishing of books. Its publication is interesting on another account, — as having been the means of introducing him to his first pastoral charge. The incumbent of Fordham in Essex having been ejected from his living by the committee for purging the church of scandalous ministers, Owen was invited by the same committee to occupy the vacant parish. Not long after his removal to Fordham, he was married to a lady of the name of Rooke. But nearly all the information that here descended to us regarding this union, from the earlier biographies, amounts to this, — that the lady bore to him eleven children, all of whom, except one daughter, died in early youth. This only daughter became the wife of a Welsh gentleman; but the union proving unhappy, she "returned to her kindred and to her father's house," and soon after died of consumption.

This period of Owen's early pastorate appears to have been one of the happiest of his life. Fordham is a secluded village, overhanging the fertile and pleasing valley of the Stour, which divides Suffolk from Essex. Its inhabitants, at the present day, number about seven hundred; but in the days of Owen they could not have been by any means so numerous. In this retreat, and surrounded by a not very dense rural population,[17] he was allowed to pursue in peace the quiet duties of a country parish, and knew nothing as yet of those more public and distracting responsibilities which he ever undertook with reluctance, and which he appears to have usually renounced with satisfaction.

---

17 We are indebted for this information regarding the first scene of Owen's ministry to the Rev. Alexander Anderson, pastor of a Baptist Church, Colchester; who also informs us that the signature of Owen is still to be seen in the parochial parish register at Fordham (four miles distant), and that it has this peculiarity attached to it, that whilst all preceding it, and also succeeding, so far as he continued his examination, sign themselves "Parson," the usual designation of the time, his signature has the word "Pastor" invariably attached to it; showing that he deliberately, and from the first, "preferred the more scriptural term of 'pastor,' to the presuming designation of parson, more especially if we accept its common derivation, '*Persona ecclesiæ*.'"

II. His Pastorate

The spiritual interests of the parish having been neglected by his predecessor, he set himself with earnest system to break up the fallow ground, and to preach those truths which had still to his mind all the freshness of first love. The good Puritan practice of visiting and catechising from house to house gave him a large place in the affections of his people, as well as revealed to him the measure of their Christian intelligence; while his solid preaching soon gathered around him the inhabitants of his own parish, and even allured multitudes across the borders of the neighbouring parishes to listen to his weighty words. Like Baxter at Kidderminster, he was ere long cheered by witnessing one of those widespread and enduring reformations which have never followed on any agency save the earnest preaching of "Christ crucified."

The productions of his pen at this period indicate the current of his thoughts, and the liveliness of his evangelic zeal. The first of these is entitled, "The Duty of Pastors and People Distinguished," and was published in 1643. Its main design is to "describe the means to be used by the people of God, distinct from church officers, for the increasing of divine knowledge in themselves and others," and to show how "the sacred calling may retain its ancient dignity, though the people of God be not deprived of their Christian liberty."[18] It bears internal evidence of having been drawn from him by the unscriptural assumptions of those ecclesiastics who thought to place their interdict on every thing like the agency of private members in the church, though there are particular passages aimed at those fiery persons who sought to introduce into the church the spirit of a wild democracy, and whose mode of making "all the Lord's people prophets," was to dispense with the inestimable benefits of a stated ministry. As it is the earliest, so it is one of the most useful of Owen's smaller treatises, and is remarkable for its skilful harmonizing of authority with liberty. How much of his axiomatic sagacity there is in the following sentence: "Truth revealed

---

18 Preface, p. 10, ed. 1644.

to any, carries with it an immovable persuasion of conscience that it ought to be published and spoken to others!"[19] And how much of wise restraint and rebuke in this: "Let not them who despise a faithful, painful minister in public, flatter themselves with hope of a blessing in private. Let them pretend what they will, they have not equal respect unto all God's ordinances!"[20] If Burnet's "Pastoral Care" and Baxter's "Reformed Pastor" may be named as the guides and counsellors of the ministers of that age, this, tractate might well have been placed beside them as the handbook of the people.[21]

We still trace the signs of the busy pastor in his next publication, which is entitled, "The Principles of the Doctrine of Christ Unfolded, in Two Short Catechisms;" the first being intended for young persons, the second for adults, and as an aid to parents in domestic instruction. We are reminded, as we look on the stalworth Puritan, who is soon to mingle in the great theological discussions of the day, thus preparing "milk for babes," of Johnson's admiring sentence on Isaac Watts: "Providing instruction for all ages, from those who were lisping their first lessons, to the enlightened readers of Malebranche and Locke."[22]

During these years of his laborious and unostentatious pastorate, the solid reputation of Owen was extending, and on April 29, 1646, he was appointed to preach before Parliament, on occasion of its monthly fast. The discourse is founded on Acts xvi. 9, " A vision appeared to Paul in the night: there stood

---

19 P. 38.

20 P. 49.

21 Owen quotes with approbation (p. 54) the judgment and practice of the Church of Scotland, as expressed in their Act of Assembly at Edinburgh, anno 1641. "Our Assembly also commandeth *godly conference* at all occasional meetings, or as God's providence shall dispose, as the Word of God commandeth, providing none invade the pastor's office, to preach the Word, who are not called thereunto by God and his church."

22 Lives of the Poets, iv. 164.

II. His Pastorate

a man of Macedonia, and prayed him, saying, Come over into Macedonia, and help us;" and is written in a style of popular eloquence by no means characteristic of the usual strain of Owen's writings. The thanks of the House were conveyed to Owen by Mr Fenner and Sir Philip Wentworth, and the discourse commanded to be printed. The evangelic zeal of the pastor of Fordham breaks forth, towards the close, in behalf of those parts of the empire which were destitute of religious instruction, and especially in behalf of his ancestral country, Wales: "When manna fell in the wilderness from the hand of the Lord, every one had an equal share. I would there were not now too great an inequality when secondarily in the hand of man, whereby some have all, and others none; some sheep daily picking the choice flowers of every pasture, — others wandering upon the barren mountains, without guide or food."[23] The glowing terms in which he dedicates his sermon to the Long Parliament, as "most deservedly celebrated through the whole world, and to be held in everlasting remembrance by all the inhabitants of this island," have drawn forth the disapprobation of some. But what contemporary opinion has been more justified by the calm judgment of later history? What English Parliament ever bore upon its roll such a list of patriots, or surrounded the immunities of the people with such constitutional guards? Even the grudging concession of Hume goes so far as to say that their conduct, with one exception, was such as "to entitle them to praise from all lovers of liberty."[24]

Not long after this, Owen's pastoral connection with Fordham was brought to a close. The "sequestered incumbent" whose place he had occupied died, and the right of presenting to the living having in this way reverted to the patron, it was given to another. The event became the occasion of introducing him to a wider sphere. The people of Coggeshall, an import-

---

23 Owen's Sermons, fol. ed., p. 214.

24 Hume's History of England, vi. ch. li. Vaughn's Stuart Dynasty, ii. 74.

ant market-town of Essex, about five miles distant, no sooner received the tidings of his deprivation than they sent a pressing invitation to him to become their minister, — an invitation which the patron, the Earl of Warwick, immediately confirmed. Unlike Fordham, this new charge had previously been diligently cultivated by a succession of faithful ministers; so that his work was not so much to lay the foundation as to build. He soon beheld himself surrounded by a congregation of nearly two thousand people, whose general religious consistency and Christian intelligence were a delight to his heart, and whose strong attachment to him subsequent events gave them abundant opportunities of testifying.[25]

Contemporaneously with these outward changes in Owen's position, considerable changes also took place in his opinions on church government. His removal to Coggeshall is named as the period at which he renounced Presbytery; and the order of his church there is said to have been brought into a closer conformity with the Independent or Congregational model.

There were principles, however, retained by Owen, both on the subject of the ruling elder and of synods, — as we shall have occasion to show in noticing some of his later writings, — which prove that his Congregationalism was of a somewhat modified character, and which a moderate Presbyterian of our own times, though not vaunting as identical with his views, would yet hail as evidence that the gulf between himself and the Congregationalist is not impassable. But the Presbyterians of Owen's early days in general went much farther than those of the present age; and we deem it not the least of his honours that he refused to follow in their course. Not that we have any sympathy with those terms of unqualified censure with which the Presbyterians of that age have too often been characterized. During the period of their brief supremacy, they accomplished much for England. In proportion as we value those noble statements of doctrine, the Westminster Confession and Catechisms,

---

25 Wood's Athen. Oxon., iv. 100.

II. His Pastorate

must we be grateful to the Presbyterians, who took so prominent and cordial a part in those deliberations which produced them. Well-informed and candid men of other religious parties have not been slow to admit that those districts of England which were brought under a Presbyterian pastorate and polity, made visible progress in Christian intelligence and piety; and many of those measures which were adopted by them in opposition to Cromwell, and which have often been ascribed to hostility to liberty, were, in fact, honest endeavours on their part to restore a constitutional government. But the intolerant spirit which animated them at this particular juncture is neither to be extenuated nor denied.

Having recently risen to power, they had become dazzled by the dream of an impracticable uniformity, and, as Baxter, himself a Presbyterian, complains, had shown too great a readiness to invoke to their aid in realizing this ambitious dream the arm of secular power. The endless diversity of opinion which the growing liberty and the general ferment at the public mind had occasioned was regarded by them as evidence of the dangers of unlimited toleration, and they imagined that amid such discordant sounds truth must be indistinguishable, and even perish from the earth. Owen's mind had, meanwhile, far advanced beyond these narrow views, and risen above these imaginary fears. He had boundless confidence in the vitality of truth, — strong convictions of the power of its own spiritual weapons, and of the utter impotence of every other: and while so many of those with whom he hitherto been associated saw only, in the mingled light and darkness, the approach of night, he hailed in them the hopeful twilight which was to grow into perfect day. In a "Country essay for the practice of church government," prefixed to his sermon before Parliament, he repeatedly condemns all enforced conformity and punishment of heretical opinions by the sword. "Heresy," says he, "is a canker, but it is a spiritual one; let it be prevented by spiritual means:

cutting off men's heads is no proper remedy for it."[26] That Owen should have renounced Presbytery, in the intolerant and repulsive form in which it was at this time presented to him, is not to be wondered at; but that he recoiled equally far at every point from all the essential and distinctive principles of that form of church government is a statement which many have found it more difficult to believe. At the same time, no reasonable doubt can be entertained that the government of Owen's church at Coggeshall was decidedly Congregational; and if that church in any degree corresponded with the counsels which Owen addressed to it in his next publication, it must have been pre-eminently one of those to which Baxter alludes in that honourable testimony, "I saw a commendable care of serious holiness and discipline in most of the Independent churches." The publication to which we refer is "Eshcol; or, Rules of Direction for the Walking of the Saints in Fellowship according to the order of the Gospel, 1647." The rules are arranged into two parts, — those which relate to the duty of members to their pastors, and those which specify the duties of members to each other. They are designed to recall men from debates about church order to the serious, humble performance of those duties which grow out of their common fellowship in the gospels. Amid its maxims of holy wisdom it would he impossible to discover whether Owen was a Congregationalist or a Presbyterian.

"Eshcol" was the work of Owen as a pastor; in the following year he was once more to appear as a theologian and Christian polemic, in a work on which he had long been secretly engaged, — "*Salus Electorum, Sanguis Iesu*; or, the Death of Death in the Death of Christ." The great subject of this treatise is the nature and extent of the death of Christ, with especial reference to the Arminian sentiments on the latter subject. It is dedicated to the Earl of Warwick, the good patron who had introduced Owen to Coggeshall, and warmly recommended by two Presbyterian ministers as "pulling down the rotten house

---

26 Owen's Sermons, fol. ed., p. 229.

II. His Pastorate

of Arminianism upon the head of those Philistines who would uphold it."[27] Owen himself makes no secret of having devoted to it immense research and protracted meditations. He had given it to the world after a more than seven-years serious inquiry, with a serious perusal of all that the wit of man, in former or latter days, had published in opposition to the truth.[28] It is not without good reason therefore, that he claims a serious perusal in return: "Reader, if thou art as many in this pretending age, a sign or title gazer, and comest into books as Cato into the theatre, to go out again, — thou hast had thy entertainment: farewell." The characteristic excellencies of Owen's mind shine out in this work with great lustre, — comprehension and elevation of view, which make him look at his subject in its various relations and dependencies, united with the most patiently minute examination of its individual parts, — intellectual strength, that delights to clear its way through impeding sophistries and snares, — soundness of judgment, often manifesting, even in his polemical writings, the presence and power of a heavenly spirit, and "expressing itself in such pithy and pregnant words of wisdom, that you both delight in the reading, and praise God for the writer."[29] Owen does not merely touch his subject, but travels through it with the elephant's grave and solid step, if sometimes also with his ungainly motion; and more than any other writer makes you feel, when he has reached the end of his subject, that he has also exhausted it.

In those parts of the present treatise in which he exhibits the glorious union and co-operation of the Father, Son, and Holy Spirit, in the work of redemption, and represents the death of Christ as part of the divine plan which infallibly secures the bringing of many sons unto glory, he has shown a mastery

---

27 The names of these ministers are, Stanley Gower and Richard Byfield.

28 Address to the Reader.

29 Gower's Attestation.

of argument and a familiarity with the subject-matter of revelation, that leave even the kindred treatise of Witsius far behind. Many modern Calvinists have, indeed, expressed a doubt whether, in thus establishing the truth, he has yet established the whole truth; and whether his masterly treatise would not have more completely exhibited the teaching of Scripture on the relations of the death of Christ, had it shown that, in addition to its more special designs, and in harmony with them, it gave such satisfaction to the divine justice as to lay a broad and ample foundation for the universal calls of the Gospel. It is quite true that the great object of the book is to prove that Christ died for the elect only; and yet there are paragraphs in which Owen, in common with all Calvinists worthy of the name who hold the same view, argues for the true internal perfection and sufficiency of the sacrifice of Christ, as affording a ground for the indiscriminate invitations of the Gospel, in terms as strong and explicit as the most liberal Calvinist would care to use.[30] This great work was the occasion of much controversy; and it is worthy of especial notice that it was the first production that turned towards Owen the keen eye of Richard Baxter, and brought the two great Puritans at length to measure arms.[31]

---

30   Book iv. ch. i. sect. 1.

31   The controversy was protracted through many treatises, particularly on the side of Baxter, in the appendix to his "Aphorisms on Justification," in his "Confession of Faith," and in his "Five Disputations of Right to the Sacraments;" and, on Owen's part, in a small treatise, "Of the Death of Christ," &c., and in the close of his "*Vindiciæ Evangelicæ.*" Various technical distinctions were introduced in the progress of the discussion, — such as, whether the death of Christ was, "*solutio ejusdem,* or only *tantundem.*" The frequent bandying of this and similar scholastic phrases, in the theological controversies of the age, caught the ear of the author of "Hudibras," and served him at times as matter for ridicule:—

"The question, then, to state it first,
Is, Which is better, or which is worst, —
Synod or bears? Bears I avow
To be the worst, and synods thou;
But to make good th' assertion,

II. His Pastorate

Eventful and anxious years were now passing over the land, in which the long struggle between prerogative and popular right continued to be waged with various success; and at length Owen beheld war brought almost to his door. The friends of Charles, having suddenly risen in Essex, had seized on Colchester, and imprisoned a committee of Parliament that had been sent into Essex to look after their affairs. Lord Fairfax, the leader of the Parliament's forces, had in consequence been sent to recover Colchester and deliver the committee, and for nearly ten weeks maintained a strict siege before its walls. Coggeshall, being not far distant, was chosen as the head quarters of the general; and intercourse having been begun between him and Owen, it became the foundation of a lasting friendship, which, we shall soon find, was not without important fruits. At the close of the ten weeks' siege, of which Owen describes himself as having been an "endangered spectator," he preached two sermons; the one to the army at Colchester on a day of thanksgiving for its surrender, and the other at Rumford to the Parliamentary committee on occasion of their deliverance. These were afterwards published as one discourse on Hab. i. 1–9.[32]

But in the course of a few months, Owen was called to officiate in circumstances unspeakably more critical. Charles I. had been brought to trial before the High Court of Justice, on the charge of being a traitor, tyrant, and murderer; and, in execution of its daring judgment, beheaded before the gates of Whitehall. On the day following this awful transaction, Owen preached by command before Parliament; and the manner in which he discharged this unsought and perilous duty, it has been not unusual to represent as one of the most vulnerable points in his public life. His sermon, which is entitled, "Righteous Zeal Encouraged

---

> Thou say'st th' are really all one.
> If so, not worst; for if th' are *idem*,
> Why then *tantundem dat tantidem.*"
> Canto iii.

32 Neal, iii. 407. Asty, p. viii.

by Divine Protection," is founded on Jer. xv. 19, 20, "I will make thee unto this people a fenced brasen wall; and they shall fight against thee, but they shall not prevail against thee: for I am with thee to save thee, and to deliver thee, saith the Lord," — a passage which obviously gave him ample opportunity for commenting on recent events. It is remarkable, however, that there is throughout a systematic and careful confining of himself to general statements, the most explicit allusion to the event of which, doubtless, every mind at the moment was full, being in that two edged sentence, "To those that cry, give me a king, God can give him in his anger; and from those that cry, Take him away, he can take him away in his wrath;" and the charge founded on this constrained silence, from the days of Owen to our own, is that of selfish and cowardly temporizing. Even one eminent Scottish historian, dazzled, we presume, by the picture of his own Knox, with Bible in hand, addressing Mary, and of other stern presbyters rebuking kings, imagines one of these to have occupied the place of Owen, and with what fearless fidelity he would have addressed those august commoners, "even though every hair of their heads had been a spear pointed at his breast."[33]

But is there not a considerable amount of undue severity in all this? In all likelihood those who had demanded this service of Owen blamed him for an opposite reason, and hoped that this theologian of high renown and untainted reputation would, in the hour of their extremity, have surrounded their daring act with something more than the dubious sanction of his ominous silence. But to ascribe his silence to cowardice, is to assume that he secretly regarded the destruction of Charles as an indefensible act of crime. And was this necessarily Owen's judgment? It was surely possible that, while believing that the party which had brought Charles to the scaffold had violated the letter of the constitution, he may also have believed that it was in righteous punishment of one whose whole career as a

---

33 M'Crie's Miscellaneous Works, p. 502.

II. His Pastorate

monarch had been one long conspiracy against it, and who had aimed, by fourteen years of force and perfidy, to establish despotism upon the ruins of popular liberty. He may have thought that treason was as possible against the constitution as against the crown, and to the full as criminal; and that where a king rejected all government by law, he could no longer be entitled to the shelter of irresponsibility. He may have looked upon the death of Charles as the last resource of a long-tried patience, — the decision of the question, Who shall perish? the one, or the million? We do not say that these were actually Owen's sentiments, but it is well known that they were the thoughts of some of the purest and loftiest minds of that earnest age; and if Owen even hesitated on these points, on which it is well known Milton believed,[34] then silence was demanded, not only by prudence, but by honesty, especially in a composition which he himself describes as, "like Jonah's gourd, the production of a night."

Whatever opinion may be formed of Owen's conduct in the matter of the sermon, there are few, we imagine, that will not look on the publication of his "Discourse on Toleration," annexed to the sermon, and presented to the Parliament along with it, as one of the most honourable facts in the public life of this great Puritan. The leading design of this essay is to vindicate the principle, that errors in religion are not punishable by the civil magistrate, with the exception of such as in their own nature, not in some men's apprehensions, disturb the order of society.[35] To assert that this great principle, which is the foundation-stone of religious liberty, was in any sense the discovery of Owen, or of that great party to which he belonged, is to display a strange oblivion of the history of opinions. Even in the writings of some of the earliest Reformers, such as Zwingle, the principle may be found stated and vindicated with all the clear-

---

34 Milton's Tenure of Kings and Magistrates, Defence of the People of England.

35 Owen's Sermons, fol. ed., p. 291.

ness and force with which Owen has announced it;[36] and Principal Robertson has satisfactorily proved, that the Presbyterian church of Holland was the first among the churches of the Reformation formally to avow the doctrine, and to embody and defend it in its authoritative documents.[37] Nor is it matter of mere conjecture, that it was on the hospitable shores of Holland, and in the bosom of her church, that English fugitives first learned the true principles of religious liberty, and bore them back as a precious leaven to their own land.[38] It is enough to say of Owen and his party, that in their attachment to these principles they were greatly in advance of their contemporaries; and that the singular praise was theirs, of having been equally zealous for toleration when their party had risen to power, as when they were a weak and persecuted sect. And when we consider the auspicious juncture at which Owen gave forth his sentiments on this momentous subject, his influence over that great religious party of which he was long the chief ornament and ruling spirit, as well as the deference shown to him by the political leaders and patriots of the age, it is not too much to say, that when the names of Jeremy Taylor and Milton, and Vane and Locke are mentioned, that of John Owen must not be forgotten, as one of the most signal of those who helped to fan and quicken, if not to kindle, in England, that flame which, "by God's help, shall never go out;" who, casting abroad their thoughts on the public mind when it was in a state of fusion and impressibility, became its preceptors on the rights of conscience, and have contributed to make the principles of religious freedom in England familiar, omnipresent, and beneficent, as the light or the air.

On the 19th of April we find Owen once more summoned to preach before Parliament, the chiefs of the army being also

---

36   Hess, Life of Zwingle, pp. 148, 159–161. M'Crie's Miscellaneous Works, p. 473.

37   Robertson's Charles I., iv. 131.

38   M'Crie's Miscellaneous Works, p. 474.

present; on which occasion he preached his celebrated sermon, "On the Shaking of Heaven and Earth," Heb. xii. 27. Oliver Cromwell was present, and probably for the first time heard Owen preach. Ere the sermon was completed, Cromwell had formed a resolution which the following day gave him an opportunity of executing. Owen having called at the house of General Fairfax, to pay his respects to him in remembrance of their recent intercourse at Colchester, was informed by the servants that the general was so indisposed that he had already declined to receive the visits of several persons of quality. The pastor of Coggeshall, however, sent in his name; and while waiting, Cromwell and many other officers entered the room. Owen's tall and stately figure soon caught the eye of Cromwell as the person whom he had heard preach with so much delight yesterday; and going up to him, he laid his hands upon his shoulders, and said to him familiarly, "Sir, you are the person I must be acquainted with." Owen modestly replied, "That will be much more to my advantage than yours." To which Cromwell returned, "We shall soon see that;" and taking Owen by the hand, led him into the garden, and made known to him his intention to depart for Ireland, and his wish that Owen should accompany him as chaplain, and also to aid him in investigating and setting in order the affairs of the University of Dublin. To this unexpected proposal Owen naturally objected the claims of his church at Coggeshall; but Cromwell reminding him that he was about to take his younger brother, whom he dearly loved, as standard-bearer in the same army, would not listen to a refusal. He even wrote to the church at Coggeshall urging their consent; and when they showed themselves even more averse to the separation than their pastor, Cromwell rose from entreaties to commands; and Owen, with the advice of certain ministers whom he consulted, was at length induced to make slow preparations for the voyage.[39]

---

39 Asty, pp. ix., x.

In the interval between these arrangements and his departure for Ireland, we discover Owen once more preaching before the officers of state and the House of Commons, on occasion of the destruction of the Levellers;[40] and about the middle of August we find the army ready to embark for Ireland. On the day before the embarkation it presented one of those characteristic pictures which are almost without a parallel in the history of nations. The entire day was devoted to fasting and prayer; — three ministers in succession, among whom we cannot doubt was Owen, solemnly invoked the divine protection and blessing; after which Colonels Gough and Harrison, with Cromwell himself, expounded certain pertinent passages of Scripture. No oath was heard throughout the whole camp, the twelve thousand soldiers spending their leisure hours in reading their Bibles, in the singing of psalms, and in religious conferences. Thus was trained that amazing armament, to whom victory seemed entailed, — whose soldiers combined the courage of the ancient Roman with the virtues of the private citizen, and have been well described as "uniting the most rigid discipline with the fiercest enthusiasm, and moving to victory with the precision of machines, while burning with the wildest fanaticism of crusaders."[41] There were elements at work here that have seldom gone to the composition of armies. "Does the reader look upon it all as madness? Madness lies close by, as madness does to the highest wisdom in man's life always; but this is not mad! This dark element, it is the mother of the lightnings and the splendours; it is very sure this?"[42]

It is no task of ours to follow the course of Cromwell in his rapid and terrible campaign, in which he descended upon Ireland "like the hammer of Thor," and by a few tremendous and

---

40 The title of the sermon was, "Human Power Defeated," Ps. lxxvi. 5.

41 Whitelock, p. 434. Neal, iv. 4–6. Macaulay's History of England, i. p. 121.

42 Carlyle's Cromwell, i. p. 341.

II. His Pastorate

almost exterminating strokes, as before the walls of Drogheda, spread universal terror throughout the garrisons of Ireland, saving more blood than if he had adopted a more feeble and hesitating course. His policy in Ireland finds its explanation in two circumstances, — the impression that he had come as the instrument of a just God to avenge the innocent blood of more than a hundred thousand Protestants, — and the conviction that, in repressing a rebellion which threatened the existence of the infant Commonwealth, the "iron hand," though the least amiable, was the most merciful, and would save the necessity of a wider though more prolonged vengeance.[43] But our business is with Owen, whom we find meanwhile employed within the friendly walls of Dublin in preaching to "a numerous multitude of as thirsting people after the gospel as ever he conversed with," investigating the condition of the university, and devising measures for its extension and efficiency. His preaching was "not in vain," while his representations to Parliament led to measures which raised the university from its half-ruinous condition, and obtained for it some of its most valuable immunities.[44] In the course of nine months, Cromwell, whose career in Ireland had been that of the lightning followed by the shower, terrific yet beneficent, returned to England to receive the thanks of the Parliament and the people, and to be appointed General-in-chief of the armies of the Commonwealth; and Owen, mourning over the fact "that there was not one gospel preacher for every walled town in Ireland,"[45] was restored to his rejoicing flock at Coggeshall.

But the release which he was to enjoy was short. Cromwell had scarcely returned from Ireland, when the state of Scotland demanded his presence. That nation, which had begun the re-

---

43 D'Aubigné's Protector, ch. vi.

44 Orme, p. 88.

45 Sermon on the Steadfastness of Promises, and the Sinfulness of Staggering, preached before Parliament after his return from Ireland, on a day of humiliation, Rom. iv. 20.

sistance to the tyranny of the Stuarts, and to the worse tyranny of Rome, had almost unanimously disapproved of the death of Charles, and now looked with jealousy and hostility upon the government of the Commonwealth. They had actually invited Charles from the midst of his debaucheries of Breda to become their king; and, deceived by his signing of the Covenant, were now meditating an attempt to restore him to his father's throne. In all this Cromwell saw, on the part of the best of the Scottish people, an honest and misguided zeal, which was aiming substantially at the same ends as himself; but he saw in it not the less the most imminent danger to the liberty, religion, and morality of England, and hastened to assert and establish in Scotland the authority of the Commonwealth. Simultaneously with this, an order passed the Commons requiring Joseph Caryl and John Owen to attend on the Commander-general as ministers;[46] and Owen was thus a second time torn away from his pastoral plans and studious toils to the society of camps, and the din and carnage of sieges and battlefields. Cromwell's motives for thus surrounding himself with the great preachers of his age have been variously represented, according to the general theory that has been formed of his character. Believing as we do in his religious sincerity, we cannot doubt that he felt, like other religious men, the powerful attraction of their intercourse. There was sound policy, besides, in seeking by this means to convince an age remarkable for its religious earnestness that he enjoyed the confidence and friendship of the chiefs of the religious world; and hence we find him at a later period securing the presence of John Howe at Whitehall, and aiming by repeated efforts to subdue the jealous penetration of Baxter. This latter motive, we cannot doubt, had its own influence in inducing him to take Caryl and Owen with him to Scotland; and it is very probable, moreover, that, with all his passion for theological polemics, he foresaw that, in his anticipated discussions with the Scottish clergy, he would be all the better of these Puritan chiefs to help

---

46 Wood's Athen. Oxon., iv. 98.

II. His Pastorate

him at times in untying the Gordian knots which they were sure to present to him.

We are able to trace but a few of the steps of Owen in Scotland. He appears to have joined Cromwell at Berwick, where he preached from the text, Isa. lvi. 7, "For mine house shall be called an hour of prayer for all people;" and, as we conclude from a letter of Cromwell's,[47] assisted, with "some other godly ministers," in drawing up a reply to the Declaration of the General Assembly, which had already been sent to Cromwell ere he could cross the borders. We next find him writing from Musselburgh to Lisle, one of the commissioners of the Great Seal, describing a skirmish between some of Cromwell's troops and those of "cautious" Leslie. Next, the battle of Dunbar has been fought. Cromwell is in possession of Edinburgh, but the castle still holds out against him, and the ministers of the city have sought protection within its walls. The pulpits of Edinburgh are consequently in the hands of Cromwell's preachers. Owen preached repeatedly in old St. Giles', and is listened to at first with wonder and jealousy, which gradually melt into kindlier feelings, as the multitude trace in his words a sweet savour of Christ.[48] It is the opinion of many that Owen's hand is visible in the letters which passed between Cromwell and the governor of Edinburgh castle, on the offer of the Lord-General to allow the ministers to come out and occupy their pulpits on the Sabbath-day; when, on their somewhat suspicious and sulky refusal, Cromwell addressed them in that celebrated letter of which Carlyle says, that "the Scotch clergy never got such a reprimand since they first took ordination."[49] Undoubtedly there are striking resemblances to Owen's turn of thoughts especially in the paper of "Queries," which abounds in "lumbering sentences with noble meanings." We next follow him with Cromwell to

---

47 Carlyle's Cromwell, ii. 18.

48 His second sermon, on Isa. lvi. 7, was preached at Edinburgh.

49 Carlyle's Cromwell, ii. 59.

Glasgow, where Zachary Boyd thunders against the Lord-General in the old cathedral, and Cromwell listens with calm forbearance, and where a discussion takes place between Owen and the Scottish ministers, of which the following anecdote is told:— A young Scottish minister, named Hugh Binning, not yet twenty-six years of age, so managed the dispute as to confound Owen and the other English divines. Oliver, surprised and half-pleased, inquired, after the meeting was over, who this bold young man was; and being told that his name was Binning, — "He has *bound*, well indeed," said he; "but," laying his hand on his sword, "this will loose all again." The discussion, with Binning's victory, is not improbable; but the bad pun and the braggart threat are not like Oliver, and may safely be consigned to those other "anecdotes of Cromwell at Glasgow," of which Carlyle says, that "they are not to be repeated anywhere except in the nursery."[50]

But long ere Cromwell's campaign in Scotland was over, and that last battle, in which he gained "Worcester's laureate wreath," had been fought, which drove Charles back to Breda, and reduced Scotland under the generous sway of the Commonwealth, Owen had been permitted to return to his books and to his quiet pastorate in Essex. It was only a short breathing-time, however, before his connection with Coggeshall was loosed for ever. One morning he read, to his surprise, in the newspapers of the day, the following order:— "On the 18th March 1651, the House, taking into consideration the worth and usefulness of John Owen, M.A., of Queen's College, ordered that he be settled in the deanery of Christ Church, in room of Dr Reynolds."[51] A letter soon after followed this from the principal students of Christ Church, expressing their great satisfaction at the appointment. Cromwell before this had been chosen Chancellor of Oxford. And on the 9th of September of the following year, letters from Cromwell nominated Owen vice-chancellor of the

---

50   Ibid., ii. 79.

51   Asty, p. x.

II. His Pastorate

university, and thus placed him at the head of that great and ancient seat of learning from which we have seen him, ten years before, walk forth an exile for conscience' sake.[52]

---

52 His preaching before Parliament, about the period of these appointments, appears to have been frequent. On October 24, 1651, being the day of thanksgiving of the victory of Worcester, we find him preaching his sermon entitled, "The Advantage of the Kingdom of Christ in the Shaking of the Kingdoms of the World," Ezek. xvii. 24. Next, February 6, 1652, in the Abbey Church of Westminster, on the occasion of the funeral of Henry Ireton, Lord-Deputy of Ireland, and Cromwell's son-in-law, he preached his sermon on Dan. xii. 13, — "The Labouring Saint's Dismission to Rest." Once more, October 13, 1652, on "Christ's Kingdom and the Magistrate's Power," from Dan. vii. 15, 16.

III. His Vice-Chancellorship

The office of dean of Christ Church involved in it the duty of presiding at all the meetings of the college, and delivering lectures in divinity; while that of vice-chancellor virtually committed to the hands of Owen the general government of the university. A charge of inconsistency has sometimes been brought against him, as an Independent, for accepting such offices, especially that of dean; and even some sentences of Milton have been adduced to give sanction to the complaint. But the whole charge proceeds on a mistake. It should be remembered that the University of Oxford during the Commonwealth shared in those changes which befell so many other institutions, and had ceased to be a mere appendage and buttress of Episcopacy, and that the office as held by Owen was separated from its ecclesiastical functions, and retained nothing, in fact, of Episcopacy except the name. It is quite true that the emoluments of the deanery were still drawn from the same sources as at an earlier period; but Owen, in common with many of the Independents and all the Presbyterians of his times, was not in principle opposed to the support of the teachers of religion by national funds.[53]

His scruples in accepting office in Oxford, and especially in consenting to be raised to the high position of vice-chancellor, arose from other causes; and it needed all the authority of Cromwell, and all the influence of the senate, completely to overcome them. It required him to do violence to some of his best affections and strongest predilections to tear himself away from the studious days and the happy pastorate of Coggeshall; and per-

---

53 Discourse of Toleration, Owen's Sermons, fol. ed. p. 308.

III. His Vice-Chancellorship

haps it demanded a higher pitch of resolution still to undertake the government of a university which had been brought to the very brink of ruin by the civil wars, and from which, during the intervening years, it had very partially recovered. During those years of commotion, learning had almost been forgotten for arms; and Oxford, throwing itself with a more than chivalrous loyalty into the cause of Charles, had drained its treasury, and even melted its plate, in order to retrieve his waning fortunes. The consequence had been, that at the end of the civil war, when the cause of the Parliament triumphed, many of its halls and colleges were closed; others of them had been converted into magazines for stores and barracks for soldiers; the studious habits of its youth had been completely disturbed, and the university burdened with a debt of almost hopeless magnitude. Some of the worst of these evils still remained, — others of them were only partially diminished; and when we add to this the spirit of destructive Vandalism with which a noisy party began to regard those ancient seats of learning, the licentiousness and insubordination which the students had borrowed from the armies of the Royalists, as well as the jealousy with which Owen was regarded by the secret friends of Episcopacy, and by Presbyterians who had been displaced by Cromwell from high positions in order to give place to Independents, it is easy to see that it required no common courage to seize the helm at such a moment, to grapple with such varied and formidable difficulties, and to reduce such discordant elements to peace.[54] Such was the work to which Owen now betook himself.

It is only too evident that even at the present day it requires, in the case of many, something like a mental effort against early prejudice, to conceive of this Puritan pastor occupying the lofty eminence to which he was now raised with a suitable amount of dignity and grace. Not only the author of "Hudibras," but

---

54 Neal, iii. 360, 361. Walker's Sufferings of the Clergy, pp. 122, 123, 128. Owen's *Oratio Quinta ad Academicos, anno 1657.* "*Per primum biennium vulgi fuimus et vulgaris fabula.*"

even Clarendon and Hume, have written of the Puritans in the style of caricature, and cleverly confounding them under a common name with ignorant and extravagant sectaries whom the Puritans all along condemned and disowned, have too long succeeded in representing the popular type of the Puritans as that of men of affected sanctity, pedantic and piebald dialect, sour temper, and unpolished manner. Those who indulge these ignorant mistake forget that if the Puritan preachers were thus utterly deficient in matters of taste and refinement, they had received their training at Oxford and Cambridge, and that the reflection must, therefore, in all fairness, be extended to those seminaries. They forget, moreover, as has been well remarked, that "it is more reasonable, and certainly much more generous, to form our judgment with regard to religious parties from the men among them who make their bequests to posterity, than from such as constitute the weakness of a body rather than its strength, and who die, as a matter of course, in the obscurity in which they have lived."[55]

But it is remarkable, that all the leading men among the Puritan clergy were such as, even in the matter of external grace and polish, might have stood before kings. The native majesty of John Howe, refined by intercourse with families of noble birth, and his radiant countenance, as if formed *meliore luto*, linger even in his portraits. Philip Henry, the playmate of princes, bore with him into his country parish that "unbought grace of life," which, in spite of his sterner qualities, attracted towards him the most polished families of his neighbourhood. Richard Baxter was the chosen associate of Sir Matthew Hale; and, contrary even to the popular notions of those whose sympathies are all on the side of Puritanism, Owen bore with him into public life none of the uncouth and lumbering pedantry of the recluse, but associated with his more solid qualities all the lighter graces of courtesy and taste. He is described by one contemporary as "of universal affability, ready presence and discourse, liberal,

---

55 Vaughan's Modern Pulpit, p. 87.

III. His Vice-Chancellorship

graceful, and courteous demeanour, that speak him certainly (whatsoever he be else) one that was more a gentleman than most of the clergy."[56] And Dodwell says, "His personage was proper and comely, and he had a very graceful behaviour in the pulpit, an eloquent elocution, a winning and insinuating deportment, and could, by the persuasion of his oratory, in conjunction with some other outward advantages, move and wind the affections of his auditory almost as he pleased."[57] It is with such a manner that we can conceive him to have addressed the assembled heads of colleges, when he assumed the helm at Oxford with tremulous hand, yet with firm determination to do his utmost to discharge his high stewardship.

> "I am well aware," said he, "gentlemen of the university, of the grief you must feel that, after so many venerable names, reverend persons, depositaries and preceptors of the arts and sciences, the fates of the university should have at last placed him as leader of the company who almost closes the rear. Neither, indeed, is this state of our affairs, of whatever kind it be, very agreeable to myself, since I am compelled to regard my return, after a long absence, to my beloved mother as a prelude to the duties of a laborious and difficult situation. But complaints are not remedies of any misfortune. Whatever their misfortune, groans become not grave and honourable men. It is the part of an undaunted mind boldly to bear up under a heavy burden. For, as the comic poet says, —

---

56 "Authority of the Magistrate in Religion Discussed," &c., by J. H.; whom Anthony Wood (Athen. Oxon., iv. 101) supposes to be John Humphrey.

57 Wood's Athen. Oxon., ibid. — We subjoin Wood's own caricature: "While he [Owen] did undergo the same office, he, instead of being a grave example to the university, scorned all formality, undervalued his office by going in quirpo like a young scholar, with powdered hair, snakebone bandstrings (or bandstrings with very large tassles), lawn bands, a very large set of ribbons pointed at his knees, and Spanish leather boots with large lawn tops, and his hat mostly cock'd." — Ibid. 98.

"'The life of man
is like a game at tables. If the cast
Which is most necessary be not thrown,
That which chance sends, you must correct by art.'[58]

"The academic vessel, too long, alas! tossed by storms, being almost entirely abandoned by all whose more advanced age, longer experience, and well-earned literary titles, excited great and just expectations, I have been called upon, by the partiality and too good opinion of him whose commands we must not gainsay, and with whom the most earnest entreaties to be excused were urged in vain, and also by the consenting suffrage of this senate; and, therefore although there is perhaps no one more unfit, I approach the helm. In what times, what manners, what diversities of opinion (dissensions and calumnies everywhere raging in consequence of party spirit), what bitter passions and provocations, what pride and malice, our academical authority has occurred, I both know and lament. Nor is it only the character of the age that distracts us, but another calamity to our literary establishment, which is daily becoming more conspicuous, — the contempt, namely, of the sacred authority of law, and of the reverence due to our ancestors; the watchful envy of Malignants; the despised tears and sobs of our almost dying mother, the university (with the eternal loss of the class of gownsmen, and the no small hazard of the whole institution); and the detestable audacity and licentiousness, manifestly Epicurean beyond all the bounds of modesty and piety, in which, alas! too many of the students indulge. Am I, then, able, in this tottering state of all things, to apply a remedy to this complication of difficulties, in which so many and so great heroes have, in the most favourable times, laboured in vain? I am not, gentlemen, so self-sufficient. Were I to act the part of one so impertinently disposed to flatter himself, nay, were the slightest thought of such a nature to enter my mind, I should be quite displeased with myself. I live not

---

58 Terence, Adelph. iv. 7, 21.

so far from home, nor am such a stranger to myself, I use not my eyes so much in the manner of witches, as not to know well how scantily I am furnished with learning, prudence, authority, and wisdom. Antiquity has celebrated Lucullus as a prodigy in nature, who, though unacquainted with even the duty of a common soldier, became without any difficulty an expert general; so that the man whom the city sent out inexperienced in fighting, him the army received a complete master of the art of war. Be of good courage, gentlemen. I bring no prodigies; from the obscurity of a rural situation, from the din of arms, from journeys for the sake of the gospel into the most distant parts of the island, and also beyond sea, from the bustle of the court, I have retreated unskilful in the government of the university; unskilful, also, I am come hither.

"'What madness is this, then?' you will say. 'Why have you undertaken that which you are unable to execute, far less to adorn? You have judged very ill for yourself, for the university, and for this venerable senate.' Softly, my hearers; neither hope nor courage wholly fails one who is swayed by the judgment, the wishes, the commands, the entreaties of the highest characters. We are not ourselves the sources of worthy deeds of any kind. 'He who ministereth seed to the sower,' and who from the mouths of infants has ordained strength, is able graciously to supply all defects, whether caused from without or felt within. Destitute, therefore, of any strength and boldness of my own, and of any adventitious aid through influence with the university, so far as I know or have deserved, it nevertheless remains to me to commit myself wholly to Him 'who giveth to all men liberally, and upbraideth not.' He has appointed an eternal fountain of supply in Christ, who furnisheth seasonable help to every pious endeavour, unless our littleness of faith stand in the way; thence must I wait and pray for light, for strength, and for courage. Trusting, therefore, in his graciously promised presence, according to the state of the times, and the opportunity which, through divine Providence we have obtained, — conscious integrity alone supplying the place of arts and of all embellishments, — without either a depressed or servile spirit, I address myself to this undertaking."[59]

The facts that have been preserved by Owen's biographers sufficiently prove that this inaugural address was no mere language of dignified ceremony. By infusing that tolerant spirit into his administration which he had often commended in his days of suffering, but which so many in those times forgot when they rose to power, — by a generous impartiality in the bestowal of patronage, — by an eagerness to detect modest merit, and to help struggling poverty, — by a firm repression of disorder and licentiousness, and a steadfast encouragement of studious habits and good conduct, — he succeeded, during the few years of his vice-chancellorship, in curing the worst evils of the university, and restoring it to such a condition of prosperity as to command at length even the reluctant praise of Clarendon.

Among other honourable facts, it is recorded that he allowed a society of Episcopalians to meet every Lord's day over against his own door,[60] and to celebrate public worship according to the forms of the liturgy, though the laws at that period put it in Owen's power to disperse the assembly; and there were not wanting those of a less enlarged and unsectarian spirit to urge him to such a course. In the same wise and conciliatory spirit he won the confidence of the Presbyterians, by bestowing upon their ablest men some of the vacant livings that were at his disposal, and taking counsel of them in all difficulties and emergencies. Many a poor and promising student was aided by him with sums of money, and with that well-timed encouragement which is more gratifying than silver and gold, and which, in more than one instance, was found to have given the first impulse on the road to fame. Foreign students of hopeful ability were admitted through his influence to the use of the librar-

---

59 *Oratio prima*, translated by Orme, pp. 128–131.

60 "At the house of Dr Willis the physician, not far from his own lodgings at Christchurch." — Biograph. Dict., x. 103.

ies and to free commons; and one poor youth, in whose Latin epistle, informing Owen of his necessities, he had discovered an unusual "sharpness of wit," was at once received by him as tutor into his own family.[61]

But, amid these generous and conciliatory measures, Owen knew how, by acts of wholesome severity, to put a curb upon licentiousness, and to invigorate the whole discipline of the university. At a public Act, when one of the students of Trinity College was *Terræ filius*, he stood up before the student began, and told him in Latin that he was at liberty to say what he pleased, on condition that he abstained from all profane and obscene expressions and personal reflections. The student began, but soon violated all the conditions that had been laid down to him. Owen repeatedly warned him to desist from a course so dishonouring to the university; but the youth obstinately persisting in the same strain, he at length commanded the beadles to pull him down. This was a signal for the students to interpose; on which Owen, determined that the authority of the university should not be insolently trampled on, rose from his seat, in the face of the remonstrances of his friends, who were concerned for his personal safety, drew the offender from his place with his own hand, and committed him to Bocardo, the prison of the university, — the students meanwhile standing aloof with amazement and fear at his resolution.[62] Was there not something, in this scene, of that robust physical energy which had distinguished Owen at Oxford in earlier days in bell-ringing and the leaping of bars?

But the aims of the vice-chancellor rose far above the mere attempt to restrain licentiousness within moderate bounds; — his whole arrangements were made with the anxious desire of awakening and fostering among the students the power of a living piety. His own example, as well as the pervading spirit

---

61 Asty, pp. xi., xii. Calamy's Noncon. Mem., i. 201. Wood's Fasti, ii. 788.

62 Asty, pp. xi., xii.

of his administration, would contribute much to this; and there are not wanting individual facts to show with what earnestness he watched and laboured for the religious well-being of the university. It had been customary for the Fellows to preach by turn on the afternoon of the Lord's day in St. Mary's Church; but, on its being found that the highest ends of preaching were often more injured than advanced by this means, he determined to undertake this service alternately with Dr Goodwin, the head of Magdalen College, and in this way to secure to the youth of Oxford the advantage of a sound and serious ministry. It is interesting to open, nearly two hundred years afterwards, the reminiscences of one of the students, and to read his strong and grateful testimony to the benefits he had derived from these arrangements of the Puritan vice-chancellor. We have this privilege in the "Memoir of Philip Henry, by his son." "He would often mention, with thankfulness to God," says the quaint and pious biographer, "what great helps and advantages he had then in the university, — not only for learning, but for religion and piety. Serious godliness was in reputation; and, besides the public opportunities they had, many of the scholars used to meet together for prayer and Christian conference, to the great confirming of one another's hearts in the fear and love of God, and the preparing of them for the service of the church in their generation. I have heard him speak of the prudent method they took then about the university sermons on the Lord's day, in the afternoon, which used to be preached by the fellows of colleges in their course; but that being found not so much for edification, Dr Owen and Dr Goodwin performed that service alternately, and the young masters that were wont to preach it had a lecture on Tuesday appointed them."[63]

But the combined duties of his two onerous offices at Oxford did not absorb all the energies of Owen. His mind appears to have expanded with his position, and to have shown resources that were literally inexhaustible. The few years which saw

---

63 Life and Times of Philip Henry, p. 60.

III. His Vice-Chancellorship

him the chief agent in raising the university from the brink of ruin, were those in which he was most frequently summoned by Cromwell to his councils, and in which he gave to the world theological works which would have been sufficient of themselves in the case of most men, to occupy and to recompense the energies of a lifetime. We now turn with him, then, for a little to the platform of public life, and to the toils of authorship.

On the 25th of August 1653 we again find him preaching, by command, before Parliament, on occasion of that celebrated victory over the Dutch fleet which established the reputation of the arms of the Commonwealth by sea, and paved the way for an honourable and advantageous peace with Holland. In October of the same year he was invited by Cromwell to London, to take part, along with some other ministers, in a conference on Christian union. The matter is stated in such interesting terms in one of the newspapers of the day, and, besides, affords such a valuable incidental glimpse of Cromwell's administration, that we prefer giving it in the words of that document:— "Several ministers were treated with by his Excellency the Lord-General Cromwell, to persuade them that hold Christ, the head, and so are the same fundamentals, to agree in love, — that there be no such divisions among people professing godliness as has been, nor railing or reviling each other for difference only in forms. There were Mr Owen, Mr Marshall (Presbyterian), Mr Nye (Independent), Mr Jessey (Baptist), Mr Harrison, and others; to whom the advice and counsel of his Excellency were so sweet and precious, and managed with each judgment and graciousness, that it is hoped it will much tend to persuade those that fear the Lord in spirit and truth to labour for the union of all God's people."[64]

It does not appear that any immediate practical measures resulted from this conference. The mistake, by which many such laudable attempts were defeated, was that of attempting too much incorporation was sought, when they should have

---

64 Cromwelliana, Orme, p. 109.

been satisfied with mutual Christian recognition and co-operation up to the point of agreement; and sometimes a constrained silence on matters of difference, where there should rather have been a generous forbearance. But it is wrong to speak of such conferences and communing, when they failed of their immediate object, as either useless or fruitless. To the good men who mingled in them, it must have deepened the feeling of unity even where it did not increase its manifestation, and even unconsciously to themselves must have lowered the walls of division. Nor is it without interest and instruction to remark, that the best men of that age and of the next were ever the readiest to give themselves to movements that had this aim. Owen, by the reproaches which he brought upon himself on this account from weaker brethren, showed himself to be before his age. The pure spirit of Howe, which dwelt in a region so far above the petty passions of earth, has expressed its longings to see the church made "more awful and more amiable" by union, in his essay "On Union among Protestants," and "On the Carnality of Religious Contentions." Baxter, with all his passion for dialectics, felt and owned the power of these holy attractions and longed the more for the everlasting rest, that he would there at length see the perfect realization of union.[65] And the saintly Usher, prompted in part by the sublime seasonings of Howe, actually proposed a scheme of comprehension, of which, though defective in some of its provisions, and not permitted to be realized, God doubtless said, "It was good that it was in thine heart to do it." The Puritans did more than make unsuccessful experiments of union: they expounded in their writings many of the principles on which alone it can be accomplished; and it seems now only to need a revival of religion from on high in order to accomplish what they so eagerly desired. They were the Davids

---

65 His spirit is expressed in the following tender words, with which he closed one his debates: "While we wrangle here in the dark, we are dying, and passing to the world that will decide all our controversies; and the safest passage thither is by a peaceable holiness."

III. His Vice-Chancellorship

who prepared the materials of the temple, — shall the Christian of this age be the sons of peace who shall be honoured to build?

It was in all likelihood while Owen was attending in London on the meetings of this conference, that the senate embraced the opportunity of diplomating him Doctor of Divinity. For we find it recorded by Wood in his "*Fasti Oxoniensis,*" that, "On Dec 23, John Owen, M.A., dean of Ch. Ch., and vice-chancellor of the university, was then (he being at Lond.) diplomated doct. of div." He is said in his diploma to be "*in palæstra theologia exercitatissimus, in concionando assiduus et potens, in disputando strenuus et acutus.*"[66] Owen's friend, Thomas Goodwin, president of Magdalen College, was diplomated on the same occasion; and the honoured associates are sneeringly described by Wood, after his manner, as "the two Atlases and Patriarchs of Independency."[67]

In the midst of these engagements, Dr Owen produced and published, in Latin, one of his most abstruse dissertations, — "*Diatriba de Divina Justitia,* etc.; or, the Claims of Vindicatory Justice Asserted." The principle which it is the design of this treatise to explain and establish is, that God, considered as a moral governor, could not forgive sin without an atonement, or such provision for his justice as that which is made by the sacrifice of Christ. It had fallen to his lot some months before, in certain theological discussions to which he was called by his office, "to discourse and dispute on the vindicatory justice of God, and the necessity of its exercise on the supposition of the existence of sin;" and his hurried treatment of the subject, in the brief hour which was allowed him, had the rare success of bringing many over to his views. Owen was convinced that his principle "struck its roots deep through almost the whole of theology."[68] He saw plainly that its effect, if established, was to raze

---

66   Wood's Fasti, ii. 179.

67   Wood's Athen. Oxon., iv. 98.

68   Preface, p. viii.

the very foundations of Socinian error; — yet he was grieved to find that many excellent divines, who held views in common with him on all the great truths of the evangelical system, wavered on this, and that some honoured names had lately given a new sanction to the opposite opinion; among whom were Dr Twisse of Newbury, prolocutor of the Westminster Assembly, in his *"Vindiciæ Gratiæ, Potestatis, ac Providentiæ divinæ,"* and the venerable Samuel Rutherford of St Andrew, in his *"Disputatio Scholastica de divina Providentia."*[69] This made him the more readily accede to the wishes of those who had received benefit and confirmation from his verbal exposition of the subject, that he would enter on its more orderly and deliberate investigation. We do not wonder that the future expositor of the Epistle to the Hebrews should have been strongly prompted to contend for this principle, since it seems wrought up with more than one part of that colossal argument of inspired theology.

In pursuing his argument, he evidently felt himself dazzled at times by the lustre of those interior truths to which his thoughts were turned. "Those points," he remarks, "which dwell in more intimate recesses, and approach nearer its immense fountain, the Father of light, darting brighter rays by their excess of light, present a confounding darkness to the minds of the greatest men, and are as darkness to the eyes breaking forth amidst so great light. For what we call darkness in divine subjects is nothing else than their celestial glory and splendour striking on the weak ball of our eyes, the rays of which we are not able in this life, which is but a vapour and shineth but a little, to bear."[70]

---

69   Orme, p. 153.

70. Many readers will be struck by the resemblance between this noble passage and that of Owen's greatest contemporary:—

> "Thee, Author of all being,Fountain of light, thyself invisible
> Amidst the glorious brightness where thou sittest
> Throned inaccessible; but when thou shadest
> The full blaze of thy beams, and through a cloud,
> Drawn round about thee like a radiant shrine,

In other places we can trace indications, that when he was rising to the height of his great argument, his fertile mind was revolving new treatises, which he afterwards gave to the world, and longing for the hour when he would descend from his present altitudes to those truths which bear more directly and powerfully on the spiritual life: "There are, no doubt, many other portions and subjects of our religion, of that blessed trust committed to us for our instructions on which we might dwell with greater pleasure and satisfaction of mind. Such, I mean, as afford a more free and wider scope of ranging through the most pleasant meads of the holy Scripture, and contemplating in these the transparent fountains of life and rivers of consolation; — subjects which, unencumbered by the thickets of scholastic terms and distinctions, unembarrassed by the impediments and sophisms of an enslaving philosophy or false knowledge, sweetly and pleasantly lead into a pure, unmixed, and delightful fellowship with the Father and with his Son, shedding abroad in the heart the inmost loves of our Beloved, with the odour of his sweet ointment poured forth."[71]

The usual number of replies followed the appearance of this treatise, in which Baxter once more stood forth equipped in his ready armour.

In the following year Dr Owen gave to the world another work, of much greater magnitude, extending over nearly five hundred folio pages. He has himself supplied its best description and analysis in its ample title-page, — "The Doctrine of the Saints' Perseverance Explained and Confirmed; or, the certain permanency of their acceptation with God and sanctification from God manifested and proved, from the eternal principles, the effectual causes, and the external means thereof; in the im-

---

> Dark with excessive bright thy skirts appear;
> Yet dazzle heaven, that brightest seraphim
> Approach not, but with both wings veil their eyes."
> Par. Lost., book iii. 374–382.

71 Preface, p. xx.

mutability of the nature, decrees, covenant, and promises of God; the oblation and intercession of Jesus Christ; the promises, exhortations, and threats of the Gospel: improved in its genuine tendency to obedience and consolation." The work was immediately called forth by the "Redemption Redeemed" of John Goodwin, an Arminian writer, to whom Owen allows nearly all the most brilliant qualities of a controversialist, except a good cause. He describes him as not only clothing every conception of his mind with language of a full and choice significance, but also trimming and adorning it with all manner of signal improvements that may render it keen or pleasant, according to his intendment and desire, and happily applies to him the words of the Roman poet:—

> *Monte decurrens velut amnis, imbres*
> *Quem super notas aluêre ripas,*
> *Fervet, immensusque ruit profundo*
> *Pindarus ore."*

The treatise, however, would be almost as complete were every part of it that refers to Goodwin expunged, and undeniably forms the most masterly vindication of the perseverance of the saints in the English tongue. Even Goodwin, with all his luxuriant eloquence, is sadly shattered when grasped by the mailed hand of the great Puritan.

> *"Luxuriant artus, effusaque sanguine laxo*
> *Membra natant."*

The style of argument is much more popular than that of the former treatise; partly because of the insinuating rhetoric of his adversary, and also because Owen knew that Arminian sentiments had found their way into many of the churches, and that if he was to convince the people, he must write for the people. The following weighty sentence refers to his avoidance of philosophical terms and scholastic forms of argument, and is worthy of Owen's sanctified wisdom: "That which we account

III. His Vice-Chancellorship 53

our wisdom and learning may, if too rigorously attended, be our folly: when we think to sharpen the reason of the Scripture, we may straiten the efficacy of the spirit of it. It is oftentimes more effectual in its own liberty, than when restrained to our methods of arguing; and the weapons of it keener in their own soft breathing, than when sharpened in the forge of Aristotle."[72]

No part of this elaborate work is more characteristic of Dr Owen than his preface to the reader, which extends over forty folio pages, until you begin to fear that "the gate shall become wider than the city." It contains an account of the treatment which the doctrine had received from the first Christian century to his own; and in its pages, which are literally variegated with Greek and Latin citations, displays an immense research. But what most surprises the reader, is to find the Doctor, when about the middle of his way, deliberately turning aside to discuss with Dr Hammond the genuineness of the Epistles of Ignatius, and to weigh the evidence which they would afford, on the supposition of their genuineness, for a primitive Episcopacy. One is tempted to trace a resemblance between the theological writing of those times and their modes of journeying. There was no moving in those days with all possible directness and celerity to the goal. The traveller stopped when he pleased, diverged where he pleased, and as often as he pleased, whenever he wished to salute a friend or to settle a controversy. — The work is dedicated to Cromwell. The strong language in which Owen speaks of his religious sincerity is interesting, as showing the estimate which was formed of the Protector's character by those who had the best opportunities of judging regarding it.[73]

---

72 Epistle Dedicatory to the Heads of Colleges, etc., at Oxford, p. 8.

73 "In the midst of all the changes and mutations which the infinitely wise providence of God doth daily effect in the greater and lesser things of this world, as to the communication of his love in Jesus Christ, and the merciful, gracious distribution of the unsearchable riches of his grace, and the hid treasures thereof purchased by his blood, he knows no repentance. Of both these you have had full experience. And though your concernment in

The mention of Cromwell's name naturally brings us back to public events, and to an occurrence which, more than almost any other in Owen's life, laid him open to the reproaches of his enemies. Cromwell having dissolved the Long Parliament in the end of 1653, had a few months after issued writs for a new election. The university of Oxford was empowered to return one member to this Parliament, and Dr Owen was elected. That he did not evince any decided unwillingness to accept this new office may be presumed for the fact that he at once took his seat in the House, and continued to sit until the committee of privileges, on account of his being a minister of religion, declared his election annulled. His systematic detractors have fastened on this part of his conduct with all the instinct of vultures, and even his friends have only ventured, for the most part, on a timid and hesitating defence. Cawdrey and Anthony Wood, not satisfied with commenting on the fact of his seeming eagerness to grasp at civil power, accuse him, on the authority of public rumour, of refusing to say whether he was a minister or not, — a charge which he left at first to be answered by its own absurdity, but which, on finding some actually crediting it, he repelled with a pardonable amount of vehement indignation, declaring it to be "so remote from any thing to give a pretence or colour to it, that I question whether Satan have impudence enough to own himself its author."[74]

But there have been others, who, while disowning all sympathy with these birds of evil omen that haunted the path of the noble Puritan, have questioned the propriety and consistency of one in Owen's circumstances, and with all his strongly-professed longings for the duties of a tranquil pastorate, so readi-

---

the former hath been as eminent as that of any person whatever in these later ages of the world, yet your interest in and acquaintance with the latter is, as of incomparably more importance in itself, so answerably of more value and esteem into you." —Dedication to His Highness, Oliver, Lord Protector.

74 Wood's Athen. Oxon., iv. 99. Pref. to Cotton's Defence, Orme, p. 112.

ly "entangling himself with the affairs of this life;" and this is certainly a more tenable ground of objection. And yet, to judge Owen rightly, we must take into view all the special elements of the case. All except those who see in ordination a mysterious and indissoluble spell, and hold the Romish figment of "once a priest, always a priest," will admit that emergencies may arise in a commonwealth when even the Christian minister may, for the sake of accomplishing the highest amount of good, place in abeyance the peculiar duties of his office, and merge the pastor in the legislator. Persons had sat with this conviction in the immediately previous Parliament; and in the last century, Dr Witherspoon, one of the purest and most conscientious of Scottish ecclesiastics, after emigrating to America, united the duties of pastor and president of Jersey College with those of a member of Congress, and was only second to Washington and Franklin in laying the foundations of the infant republic.[75] Dr Owen, in all likelihood, acted on principles similar to those which swayed the Scottish divine; and when we consider the avowed and fanatical animosity with which Oxford was regarded by a turbulent party in the state, as well as the active interest which Cromwell and his Parliament took in the religious condition of the nation, it is easy to conceive how Owen felt that he was only placing himself in a better position for watching over the well-being of the university, and for promoting the interests of religion and of religious liberty, by being there to bear his part in the deliberations regarding it. At the same time, with all these facts before us to qualify our censure, we cannot help thinking that when Owen saw the validity of his election so vehemently questioned, he would have consulted his dignity more had he declined to sit.

In the "Instrument of Government" presented by Cromwell to this Parliament, it was proposed that all who professed faith in God by Jesus Christ should be protected in their religion. In the debates which took place on this part of the instrument, its

---

75 Life of Dr Witherspoon, prefixed to works, pp. xix.–xxiii.

language was interpreted as recommending toleration to those only who were agreed on the fundamentals of Christian doctrine, — an interpretation which, there is reason to think, injuriously restricted the Protector's meaning. But the question immediately arose, what were fundamentals? and a committee of fourteen was appointed to prepare a statement for the House on this subject; who, in their turn, committed the work to fourteen divines of eminence. Owen was on this committee; and, according to Baxter, had the principal share in "wording the articles." He has been blamed for seeking to limit the blessings of toleration, on the now generally-admitted principle, that a man's religious belief ought not to be made the condition of his civil privileges. But the censure is misplaced. Owen was responsible for the correctness of his answers, — not for the use which the Parliament might make of them; but the abrupt dissolution of the Parliament which, disappointed Cromwell's expectations, prevented their being embodied in any legislative measure.[76]

About the same period Dr Owen was invited by the Protector and his Council to form part of a committee, from whose labours the cause of religion in England reaped great and permanent advantage. We refer to the commission appointed to examine candidates for ordination; whose powers soon after included the ejection of ministers and schoolmasters of heretical doctrine and scandalous life. Cromwell has been condemned for thus invading the proper functions of the church; and undoubtedly he did in this measure boldly overstep the province of the legislator; at the same time, he was right in thinking that the true greatness of his kingdom, and the stability of his government, depended on the pervading influence of religion among the people; and that it was better that the church should in this irregular manner be purged of its hirelings and money-changers, than left to sink into inefficiency and corruption.

About forty ministers, "the acknowledged flower of Puritanism," were united with a few Puritan laymen, and appointed

---

76 Baxter's own Life, p. 205. Neal, iv. 88–91.

III. His Vice-Chancellorship

to this most delicate office. Undoubtedly, the power committed to them was tremendous, and, in the hands of unscrupulous men, might have been turned to purposes the most inquisitorial and vile. But seldom has power been less abused, or the rare and incidental mischief arising from its exercise, more immeasurably outweighed by its substantial benefits. It afforded, indeed, a tempting theme for the profane genius of Hudibras, to represent the triers, in their inquiries regarding the spiritual life of candidates, as endeavouring —

> "To find, in lines of beard and face,
> The physiognomy of grace;
> And, by the sound of twang and nose,
> If all be sound within disclose;"

and high Royalists and partisans like Bishop Kennet, who had probably smarted under their investigations, in their eagerness to find matter of accusation against them, might blunder out unconscious praise. But the strong assertion of the historian of the Puritans has never been disproved, — that not a single instance can be produced of any who were rejected for insufficiency without being first convicted either of immorality, of obnoxious sentiments in the Socinian or Pelagian controversy, or of disaffection to the present government. Cromwell could, before his second Parliament, refer to the labours of the commissioners in such strong terms as these: "There has not been such a service to England since the Christian religion was perfect in England! I dare be bold to say it." And the well-balanced testimony of Baxter, given with all his quaint felicity, may be held, when we consider that he had looked on the appointment of the triers with no friendly eye, as introducing all the shadings necessary to truth: "Because this assembly of triers is most heavily accused and reproached by some men, I shall speak the truth of them; and suppose my word will be taken, because most of them took me for one of their boldest adversaries. The truth is, though some few over-rigid and over-busy

Independents among them were too severe against all that were Arminians, and too particular in inquiring after evidences of sanctification in those whom they examined, and somewhat too lax in admitting of unlearned and erroneous men that favoured Antinomianism or Anabaptism; yet, to give them their due, they did abundance of good in the church. They saved many a congregation from ignorant, ungodly, drunken teachers, — that sort of men who intend no more in the ministry then to read a sermon on Sunday, and all the rest of the week go with the people to the alehouse and harden them in sin; and that sort of ministers who either preached against a holy life, or preached as men who were never acquainted with it. These they usually rejected, and in their stead admitted of any that were able, serious preachers, and lived a godly life, of what tolerable opinion soever they were; so that, though many of them were a little partial for the Independents, Separatists, Fifth-monarchy Men, and Anabaptists, and against the Prelatists and Arminians, yet so great was the benefit above the hurt which they brought to the church, that many thousands of souls blessed God for the faithful ministers whom they let in, and grieved when the Prelatists afterwards cast them out again."[77]

Every student of the Puritan history is familiar with the magnanimous act of Howe, in recommending Fuller the historian for ordination, though a Royalist, because he "made conscience of his thoughts;"[78] and an equally high-minded and generous act of impartiality is recorded of Owen. Dr Pocock, professor of Arabic in Oxford, and one of the greatest scholars in Europe, held a living in Berks, and was about to have hard measure dealt to him by the commissioners for that county. No sooner did Owen hear of this than he wrote to Thurloe, Cromwell's secretary, imploring him to stay such rash and disgrace-

---

[77] Neal, iv. 92–97. Baxter's own Life, part i. p. 72. Orme, pp. 116–119. Vaughan's Stuart Dynasty, pp. 247–250. D'Aubigné's Protectorate, pp. 231–236.

[78] Calamy's Life of Howe, prefixed to works, p. v. Neal, iv. 97.

ful procedure. Not satisfied with this, he hastened into Berkshire in person, warmly remonstrated with the commissioners on the course which they seemed bent on pursuing, and only ceased when he had obtained the honourable discharge of the menaced scholar from farther attendance.[79]

Owen's wisdom in council involved the natural penalty of frequent consultation; and, accordingly, we find him in the following year again invited to confer with Cromwell on a subject which, in addition to its own intrinsic interest, acquires a new interest from recent agitation. Manasseh Ben Israel, a learned Jew from Amsterdam, had asked of Cromwell and his government permission for the Jews to settle and trade in England, from which they had been excluded since the thirteenth century. Cromwell, favourable to the proposal himself, submitted the question to a conference of lawyers, merchants, and divines, whom he assembled, and whom he wished to consider it in relation to the interests which they might be held respectively to represent. The lawyers saw nothing in the admission of the Jews contrary to the laws of England, some of the merchants were friendly, and some opposed; and though a living historian has described the theologians as unanimous in their opposition, they were, in fact, divided in their opinion too; some, like Mr Dury, being fierce in their opposition, even to fanaticism; and others, of whom there is reason to think Dr Owen was one, being prepared to admit them under certain restrictions. Cromwell, however, was on this subject in advance of all his counsellors, and indeed of his age, "from his shoulders and upward he was higher than any of the people," and displayed a faith in the power of truth, and an ingenuity in turning the timid objections of his advisers arguments by which they might at once have been instructed and rebuked. "Since there is a promise in holy Scripture of the conversion of the Jews," he said, "I do not know but the preaching of the gospel, as it is now in England, without idolatry or superstition, may conduce to it." "I never heard a

---

79 Biog. Dict., x. 103. Orme, p. 118.

man speak so well," was the future testimony of Sir Paul Ricaut, who had pressed into the crowd. The good intentions of the Protector were defeated; but, as an expression of his respect for the rabbi he ordered £200 to be paid to him out of the public treasury.[80]

In the midst of these public events, Owen's pen had once more been turned to authorship by the immediate command of the Council of State. The catechisms of Biddle, the father of English Socinianism, had given vogue to the errors of that school; and though various writers of ability, such as Poole and Cheynel in England, and Cloppenburg, Arnold, and Maretz on the continent, had already remarked on them, it was deemed advisable that they should obtain a more complete and sifting exposure; and Owen was selected, by the high authority we have named, to undertake the task. His *"Vindiciæ Evangelicæ,"* a work of seven hundred quarto pages, embracing all the great points of controversy between the Socinian and the Calvinist, was the fruit of this command; and was certainly a far more suitable and efficient way of extinguishing the poor heresiarch, than the repeated imprisonments to which he was subjected. Dr Owen, however, does not confine himself to the writings of Biddle, but includes in his review the Racovian catechism, which was the confession of the foreign Socinians of that age; and the Annotations of Grotius, — which, though nowhere directly teaching Socinian opinions, are justly charged by him with explaining away those passages on which the peculiar doctrines of the Gospel lean for their support, and thus, by extinguishing one light after another, leaving you at length in midnight darkness. An accomplished modern writer has pointed out a mortifying identity between the dogmas of our modern Pantheists and those of the Buddhists of India.[81] It would be easy to show that the discoveries of our modern Neologists and Rationalists are in truth the resurrection of the errors of Biddle, Smalcius,

---

80   Whitelock's Memorials, p. 673. Neal, iv. 126–128.

81   Vaughan's Age and Christianity, pp. 79–82.

III. His Vice-Chancellorship   61

and Moscorovius.[82] Again and again, in those writings, which have slumbered beneath the dust of two centuries, the student meets with the same speculations, supported by the same reasonings and interpretations, that have startled him in the modern German treatise, by their impious hardihood.

You pass into the body of this elaborate work through one of those learned porticoes in which our author delights, and in which the history of Socinianism is traced through its many forms and phases, from the days of Simon Magus to his own. No part of this history in of more permanent value than his remarks on the controversial tactics of Socinians; among which he especially notices their objection to the use of terms not to be found in Scripture; and to which he replies, that "though such terms may not be of absolute necessity to express the things themselves to the minds of believers, they may yet be necessary to defend the truth from the opposition and craft of seducers;" their cavilling against evangelical doctrines rather than stating any positive opinions of their own, and, when finding it inconvenient to oppose, or impossible to refute a doctrine, insisting on its not being fundamental. How much of the secret of error in religion is detected in the following advice: "Take heed of the snare of Satan in affecting eminency by singularity. It is good to strive to excel, and to go before one another in knowledge and in light, as in holiness and obedience. To do this *in the road* is difficult. Many, finding it impossible to emerge into any consideration by walking in the beaten path of truth, and yet not able to conquer the itch of being accounted τινες μεγαλοι, turn aside into by-ways, and turn the eyes of men to them by scrambling over hedge and ditch, when the sober traveller is not at all regarded."[83] And the grand secret of continuing in the faith grounded and settled, is expressed in the following wise sentences: "That direction in this kind which with me is *instar*

---

82   Princeton Theol. Essays, First Series. Essay on the Doctrines of the Early Socinians.

83   Preface, pp. 64, 65, quarto ed.

omnium, is for a diligent endeavour to have the power of the truths professed and contended for abiding upon our hearts; — that we may not contend for notions, but what we have a practical acquaintance with in our own souls. When the heart is cast indeed into the mould of the doctrine that the mind embraceth, — when the evidence and necessity of the truth abides in us, — when not the sense of the words only is in our heads, but the sense of the things abides in our hearts, when we have communion with God in the doctrine we contend for, — then shall we be garrisoned by the grace of God against all the assaults of men."[84]

This secret communion with God in the doctrines contended for was the true key to Owen's own steadfastness amid all those winds of doctrine which unsettled every thing but what was rooted in the soil. We have an illustration of this in the next treatise, which he soon after gave to the world, and in which he passes from the lists of controversy to the practical exhibition of the Gospel as a life-power. It was entitled, "On the Mortification of Sin in Believers;" and contains the substance of some sermons which he had preached on Rom. viii. 13. He informs us that his chief motives for this publication were, a wish to escape from the region of public debate, and to produce something of more general use, that might seem a fruit "of choice, not of necessity;" and also, "to provide an antidote for the dangerous mistakes of some that of late years had taken upon them to give directions for the mortification of sin, who, being unacquainted with the mystery of the gospel and the efficacy of the death of Christ, have anew imposed the yoke of a self-wrought-out mortification on the necks of their disciples, which neither they nor their forefathers were ever able to bear."[85] We have no means of knowing what were the treatises to which Owen here refers; but it is well known that Baxter's mind at an early period received an injurious legal bias from a work of this kind; nor is even Jer-

---

84 Preface, p. 69.

85 Preface.

emy Taylor's "Holy Living" free from the fault of minute prescription of external rules and "bodily exercise, which profiteth little," instead of bringing the mind into immediate contact with those great truths which inspire and transform whatever they touch. Nor have there been wanting teachers, in any age of the church, who

> "— do but skin and film the ulcerous place,
> While rank corruption, mining all within,
> Infects unseen."

Owen's work is a noble illustration of the Gospel method of sanctification, as we believe it to be a living reflection of his own experience. In his polemical works he was like the lecturer on the *materia medica*; but here he is the skilful physician, applying the medicine to the cure of soul-sickness. And it is interesting to find the ample evidence which this work affords, that, amid the din of theological controversy, the engrossing and perplexing activities of a high public station, and the chilling damps of a university, he was yet living near God, and, like Jacob amid the stones of the wilderness, maintaining secret intercourse with the eternal and invisible.

To the affairs of Oxford we must now return for a little. In the midst of his multifarious public engagements, and the toils of a most ponderous authorship, Owen's thoughts had never been turned from the university, and his efforts for its improvement, encouraged by the Protector and his council, as well as by the co-operation of the heads of colleges, had been rewarded by a surprising prosperity. Few things, indeed, are more interesting than to look into the records of Oxford at this period, as they have been preserved by Anthony Wood and others, and to mark the constellation of great names among its fellows and students; some of whom were already in the height of their renown, and others, with a strangely varied destiny awaiting them, were brightening into a fame which was to shed its lustre on the coming age. The presiding mind at this period was Owen himself, who, from the combined influence of station and character, obtained from all around him willing deference;[86] while associated with him in close friendship, in frequent conference, and learned research, which was gradually embodied in many folios, was Thomas Goodwin, the president of Magdalen College. Stephen Charnock had already carried many honours, and given token of that Saxon vigour of intellect and ripe devotion which were afterwards to take shape in his noble treatise on the "Divine Attributes." Dr Pocock sat in the chair of Arabic, unrivalled as an Orientalist; and Dr Seth Ward taught mathematics, already noted as an astronomer, and hereafter to be less honourably noted as so supple a timeserver, that, "amid all the changes of the times he never broke his bones." Robert Boyle had fled hither, seeking in its tranquil shades opportunity for undisturbed philosophic studies, and finding in all nature food for prayer; and one more tall and stately than the rest might be seen now amid the shady walks of Magdalen College, musing on the "Blessedness of the Righteous," and now in the recesses of its libraries, "unsphering the spirit of Plato," and amassing that learning and excogitating that divine philosophy which were soon to be transfigured and immortalized in his "Living Temple." Daniel Whitby, the acute annotator on the New Testament, and the ablest champion of Arminianism — now adorned the roll of Oxford; Christopher Wren, whose architectural genius has reared its own monument in the greatest of England's cathedrals; William Penn, the founder of Pennsylvania, and the father of the gentlest and most benignant of all our Christian sects; John Locke, the founder of the greatest school of English metaphysics, to whom was to belong the high honour of basing toleration on the principles of philosophy; William South, the pulpit satirist, whom we alternately admire for his brawny intellect and matchless style, and despise for their prostration to the lowest purposes of party; Thomas Ken, the future bishop of

---

86 "He was reckoned the brightest ornament of the university in his time." — Dr Calamy.

III. His Vice-Chancellorship

Bath and Wells, whose holiness drew forth the willing homage of the Puritans, and whose conscientiousness as a nonjuror was long after to be proved by his sufferings in the Tower; Philip Henry, now passing to the little conference of praying students, and now receiving from Dr Owen praises which only make him humbler, already delighting in those happy alliterations and fine conceits which were to be gathered from his lips by his admiring son, and embalmed in the transparent amber of that son's immortal Commentary; and Joseph Alleine, who, in his "Alarm to the Unconverted," was to produce a work which the church of God will not willingly let die, and was to display the spirit of a martyr amid the approaching cruelties of the Restoration, and the deserted hearths and silent churches of St. Bartholomew's Day.[87]

But events were beginning to transpire in the political world which were to bring Owen's tenure of the vice-chancellorship to a speedy close. He had hitherto befriended Cromwell in all his great measures, with the strong conviction that the liberties and general interests of the nation were bound up with his supremacy. He had even, on occasion of the risings of the Royalists under Colonel Penruddock in the west, busied himself in securing the attachment of the university, and in raising a troop of horse for the defence of the county, until one of his Royalist revilers, enraged at his infectious zeal, described him as "riding up and down like a spiritual Abaddon, *with white powder in his hair and black in his pocket.*"[88] But when a majority of the Parliament proposed to bestow upon Cromwell the crown and title of king, and when the Protector was evidently not averse to the entreaties of his Parliament, Owen began to suspect the workings of an ambition which, if not checked, would introduce a new tyranny, and place in jeopardy those liberties which so much had been done and suffered to secure. He therefore joined with Colonel Desborough, Fleetwood, and the majority of the army,

---

87 Wood's Fasti, part ii., pp. 169–197.

88 Orme, p. 120.

in opposing these movements, and even drew up the petition which is known to have defeated the measure, and constrained Cromwell to decline the perilous honour.[89]

Many circumstances soon made it evident, that by this bold step Dr Owen had so far estranged from himself the affection of Cromwell. Up to this time he had continued to be, of all the ministers of his times, the most frequently invited to preach on those great occasions of public state which it was usual in those days to grace with a religious service. But when, soon after this occurrence, Cromwell was inaugurated into his office as Protector, at Westminster Hall, with all the pomp and splendour of a coronation, those who were accustomed to watch how the winds of political favour blew, observed that Lockyer and Dr Manton were the divines who officiated at the august ceremonial; and that Owen was not even there as an invited guest.[90] This was significant, and the decisive step soon followed. On the 3rd of July Cromwell resigned the office of chancellor of the university; on the 18th day of the same month, his son Richard was appointed his successor; and six weeks afterwards Dr Owen was displaced from the vice-chancellorship, and Dr Conant, a Presbyterian, and rector of Exeter College, nominated in his stead.[91]

Few things in Owen's public life more became him than the manner in which he resigned the presidency of Oxford, and yielded up the academic fasces into the hands of another. He "knew both how to abound, and how to be abased." There is no undignified insinuation of ungracious usage; no loud assertion of indifference, to cover the bitterness of chagrin; no mock humility; but a manly reference to the service which he was conscious of having rendered to the university, with a generous appreciation of the excellencies of the friend to whom the

---

89 Burnet's Own Times, i. 98. Ludlow's Memoirs, p. 248. Neal, iv. 151, 152.

90 Neal, iv. 157. Orme, p. 126.

91 Neal, iv. 165.

III. His Vice-Chancellorship

government was now to be transferred. In his parting address to the university, after stating the number of persons that had been matriculated and graduated during his administration, he continues: "Professors' salaries, lost for many years, have been recovered and paid; some offices of respectability have been maintained; the rights and privileges of the university have been defended against all the efforts of its enemies; the treasury is tenfold increased; many of every rank in the university have been promoted to various honours and benefices; new exercises have been introduced and established; old ones have been duly performed; reformation of manners has been diligently studied, in spite of the grumbling of certain profligate brawlers; labours have been numberless; besides submitting to the most enormous expense, often when brought to the brink of death on your account, I have hated these limbs, and this feeble body, which was ready to desert my mind; the reproaches of the vulgar have been disregarded, the envy of others has been overcome: in these circumstances I wish you all prosperity, and bid you farewell. I congratulate myself on a successor who can relieve me of this burden; and you on one who is able completely to repair any injury which your affairs may have suffered through our inattention... But as I know not whither the thread of my discourse might lead me, I here cut it short. I seek again my old labours, my usual watchings, my interrupted studies. As for you, gentlemen of the university, may you be happy, and fare you well."[92]

---

92 Conclusion of *Oratio quinta*, translated by Orme. — Six Latin orations, delivered by Owen at Oxford while he presided over the university, have been preserved, and used to be printed at the end of the volume that contained his sermons and tracts. They will appear in the seventh volume of the present edition of Owen's works.

IV. His Retirement and Last Days

A wish has sometimes been expressed, that men who, like Owen, have contributed so largely to the enriching of our theological literature, could have been spared the endless avocations of public life, and allowed to devote themselves almost entirely to authorship. But the wisdom of this sentiment is very questionable. Experience seems to testify that a certain amount of contact with the business of practical life is necessary to the highest style of thought and authorship; and that minds, when left to undisturbed literary leisure, are apt to degenerate into habits of diseased speculation and sickly fastidiousness. Most certainly the works that have come from men of monastic habits have done little for the world, compared with the writings of those who have ever been ready to obey the voice which summoned them away from tranquil studies to breast the storms and guide the movements of great social conflicts. The men who have lived the most earnestly for their own age, have also lived the most usefully for posterity. Owen's retirement from the vice-chancellorship may indeed be regarded as a most seasonable relief from the excess of public engagement; but it may be confidently questioned whether he would have written so much or so well, had his intellect and heart been, in any great degree, cut off from the stimulus which the struggles and stern realities of life gave to them. This is, accordingly, the course through which we are now rapidly to follow him, — to the end of his days continuing to display an almost miraculous fertility of authorship, that is only equalled by that of his illustrious compeer, Richard Baxter; and, at the same time, taking no second part in

IV. His Retirement and Last Days

the great ecclesiastical movements of that most eventful age.

The next great public transaction in which we find Dr Owen engaged, was the celebrated meeting of ministers and delegates from the Independent Churches, for the purpose of preparing a confession of their faith and order, commonly known by the name of the Savoy Assembly or Synod. The Independents had greatly flourished during the Protectorate; and many circumstances rendered such a meeting desirable. The Presbyterian members of the Westminster Assembly had often pressed on them the importance of such a public and formal exposition of their sentiments. Their Independent brethren in New England had set them the example ten years before; and the frequent misrepresentations to which they were exposed, especially through their being confounded with extravagant sectaries who sheltered themselves beneath the common name of Independents, as well as the religious benefits that were likely to accrue from mutual conference and comparison of views, appeared strongly to recommend such a measure. "We confess," say they, "that from the very first, all, or at least the generality of our churches, have been in a manner like so many ships, though holding forth the same general colours, launched singly, and sailing apart and alone on the vast ocean of these tumultuous times, and exposed to every wind of doctrine, under no other conduct than that of the Word and Spirit, and their particular elders and principal brethren, without association among themselves, or so much as holding out common lights to others, whereby to know where they were."[93]

It was with considerable reluctance, however, that Cromwell yielded his sanction to the calling of such a meeting. He remembered the anxious jealousy with which the proceedings of the Westminster Assembly had been watched, and probably had his own fears that what now began in theological discussion might end in the perilous canvassing of public measures. But his scruples were at length overcome, — circulars were is-

---

[93] Confess. Pref., p. 6. Neal, iv. 173.

sued, inviting the churches to send up their pastors and delegates, and more than two hundred brethren appeared in answer to the summons. They met in a building in the Strand, which was now commonly devoted to the accommodation of the officers of Cromwell's court, but which had formerly been a convent and a hospital, and originally the palace of the Duke of Savoy, from whom it took its name. A committee, in which Owen and Goodwin evidently bore the burden of the duties, prepared a statement of doctrine each morning, which was laid before the Assembly, discussed, and approved. They found, to their delight, that "though they had been launched singly, they had all been steering their course by the same chart, and been bound for one and the same port; and that upon the general search now made, the same holy and blessed truths of all sorts which are current and warrantable among the other churches of Christ in the world, had been their lading."[94] It is an interesting fact, that, with the exception of its statements on church order, the articles of the Savoy Confession bear a close resemblance to those of the famous Confession of the Westminster divines, — in most places retaining its very words. This was a high and graceful tribute to the excellence of that noble commend. And though Baxter, irritated by the form of some of its statements,[95] wrote severely against the Savoy Assembly, yet a spirit of extraordinary devotion appears to have animated and sustained its conferences. "There was the most eminent presence of the Lord," says an eyewitness, "with those who were then assembled, that ever I knew since I had a being."[96] And, as the natural consequence of this piety, there was an enlarged charity towards other churches "holding the Head." In the preface to the Confession, which Owen is understood to have written, and from which we have already made some beautiful extracts, this

---

94 Ibid.

95 Baxter's Catholic Communion Defended, and Life, p. 104.

96 Letter from Rev. J. Forbes of Gloucester. Asty, p. xxi.

IV. His Retirement and Last Days   71

blessed temper shines forth in language that seems to have anticipated the standing-point to which the living churches of our own times are so hopefully pointing. We are reminded in one place that "the differences between Presbyterians and Independents are differences between *fellow-servants;*" and in another place, the principle is avowed, that "churches consisting of persons sound in the faith and of good conversation, ought not to refuse communion with each other, though they walk not in all things according to the same rule of church order."[97] It is well known that the Savoy Confession has never come into general use among the Independents; but there is reason to think that its first publication had the best effects; and in all likelihood the happy state of things which Philip Henry describes as distinguishing this period is referable, in part at least, to the assurance of essential unity which the Savoy Confession afforded. "There was a great change," says he, "in the tempers of good people throughout the nation, and a mighty tendency to peace and unity, as if they were by consent weary of their long clashings."[98]

What would have been the effects of these proceedings upon the policy of the Protector, had his life been prolonged, we can now only surmise. Ere the Savoy Assembly had commenced its deliberations, Oliver Cromwell was struggling with a mortal distemper in the palace of Whitewall. The death of his favourite daughter, Lady Claypole, as well as the cares of his government, had told at length upon his iron frame; and on September 3, 1658, the night of the most awful storm that had

---

97 Of the Institution of Churches, and the Order Appointed in them by Jesus Christ.

98 Neal, iv. 178. One of the few letters of Dr Owen that have been preserved has reference to this Confession. A French minister of some eminence, the Rev. Peter du Moulin, wished to attempt a French translation of so valuable a document; but before doing so, he ventured some animadversions on certain of its sentiments and expressions. Owen's reply betrays some irritation, especially at Moulin's misunderstanding and consequent misrepresentation of the passages commented on. See Appendix.

ever shaken the island, and the anniversary of some of his greatest battles, Oliver Cromwell passed into the eternal world. It is no duty of ours to describe the character of this wonderful man; but our references to Owen have necessarily brought us into frequent contact with his history; and we have not sought to conceal our conviction of his religious sincerity and our admiration of his greatness. Exaggerate his faults as men may, the hypocritical theory of his character, so long the stereotyped representation of history, cannot be maintained. Those who refuse him all credit for religion must explain to us how his hypocrisy escaped the detection of the most religious men of his times, who, like Owen, had the best opportunities of observing him. Those who accuse him of despotism must tell us how it was that England, under his sway, enjoyed more liberty than it had ever done before.[99] Those who see in his character no qualities of generous patriotism, and few even of enlarged statesmanship, must reconcile this with the fact of his developing the internal resources of England to an extent which had never been approached by any previous ruler, — raising his country to the rank of a first power in Europe, until his very name became a terror to despots, and a shield to those who, like the bleeding Vaudois in the valleys of Piedmont, appealed to his compassion.

Owen, and other leading men among the Puritans, have been represented, by writers such as Burnet, as offering up the most fanatical prayers for the Protector's recovery; and after his death, on occasion of a fast, in the presence of Richard and the

---

99   Bishop Kennet has long since given the true statement of the case in reference to the ordinances against Episcopal worship during Cromwell's government. "It is certain," says he, "that the Protector was for liberty and the utmost latitude to all parties, so far as consisted with the peace and safety of his person and government; and even the prejudice he had against the Episcopal party was more for their being Royalists than for their being of the good old church." — Neal, iv. 125. In point of fact, the ordinances were not put in execution except against such clergymen as had become political offenders. — Parr's Life of Usher, p. 75. Vaughan's Stuart Dynasty, i. 246.

IV. His Retirement and Last Days

other members of his family, as almost irreverently reproaching God for his removal. It would be too much to affirm, that nothing extravagant or extreme was spoken, even by eminently good men, at a crisis so exciting; but there is every reason to think that Owen was not present at the deathbed of the Protector at all; and Burnet's statement,[100] when traced to its source, is found to have originated in an impression of Tillotson's, who was as probably mistaken as otherwise. Vague gossip must not be received as the material of biography. At the same time, it cannot be doubted that the death of Cromwell filled Owen and his friends with profound regret and serious apprehension. His life and power had been the grand security for their religious liberties; and now by his death that security was dissolved. Cromwell during his lifetime had often predicted, "They will bring all to confusion again;" and now that his presiding hand was removed, the lapse of a little time was sufficient to show that he had too justly forecast the future. Ere we glance, however, at the rapid changes of those coming years, we must once more turn to Owen's labours as an author.

In 1657 he published one of his best devotional treatises, — "Of Communion with God the Father, Son, and Holy Ghost, each Person distinctly, in Love, Grace, Consolation, etc." It forms the substance of a series of sermons preached by him at Oxford during his vice-chancellorship, and is another evidence of his "close walk with God" during the excitements and engagements of that high official position.

---

100 Burnet's Own Times, i. 116, 117. No fanatical words are directly charged upon Owen by any of is accusers, but his extravagance is freely surmised. — Biog. Dict., x. 103. Goodwin is represented as complaining in these words, "Lord, thou hast deceived us, and we were deceived;" — words which Burnet characterizes as impudent and enthusiastic boldness; but which, if used at all, were evidently accommodated from Jer. xx. 7, and used in the sense in which the prophet himself had used them; *q.d.*, "Lord, thou hast permitted us to deceive ourselves." This may probably be taken as a specimen of the looseness of the other charges.

There is, no doubt, some truth in the remark, that he carries out the idea of distinct communion between the believer and each of the persons of the Godhead to an extent for which there is no scriptural precedent; and this arises from another habit, observable in some degree even in this devotional composition, — that of making the particular subject on which he treats the centre around which he gathers all the great truths of the Gospel; but, when these deductions have been made, what a rich treasure is this work of Owen's! He leads us by green pastures and still waters, and lays open the exhaustless springs of the Christian's hidden life with Christ in God. It is easy to understand how some parts of it should have been unintelligible, and should even have appeared incoherent to persons whose creed was nothing more than an outward badge; and therefore we are not surprised that it should have provoked the scoffing remarks of a Rational ecclesiastic twenty years afterwards;[101] but to one who possesses even a faint measure of spiritual life, we know few exercises more congenial or salutary than its perusal. It is like passing from the dusty and beaten path into a garden full of the most fragrant flowers, from which you return still bearing about your person some parts of its odours, that reveal where you have been. And those who read the book with somewhat of this spiritual susceptibility, will sympathize with the glowing words of Daniel Burgess regarding it: "Alphonsus, king of Spain, is said to have found food and physic in reading Livy; and Ferdinand, king of Sicily, in reading Quintus Curtius; — but you have here nobler entertainment, vastly richer dainties, incomparably more sovereign medicines: I had almost said, the very highest of angel's food is here set before you; and, as Pliny

---

101 Dr Sherlock, in a treatise entitled, "Discourse concerning the Knowledge of Jesus Christ, and our Union and Communion with Him," etc., 1674. To which Owen replied in "A Vindication of some Passages concerning Communion with God, from the Exceptions of Willian Sherlock, Rector of St George's, Buttolph Lane." The controversy drew a considerable number of other combatants into the field, and appears to have been protracted through a series of years. — Wood's Athen. Oxon., iv. 105, 106.

IV. His Retirement and Last Days

speaks, '*Permista deliciis auxilia*,' — things that minister unto grace and comfort, to holy life and liveliness"[102]

In the same year Owen was engaged in an important and protracted controversy on the subject of schism, which drew forth from him a succession of publications, and exposed him to the assaults of many adversaries. Foster has sarcastically remarked on the great convenience of having a number of words that will answer the purposes of ridicule or reprobation, without having any precise meaning attached to them;[103] and the use that has commonly been made of the obnoxious term, "Schism," is an illustration in point. Dominant religious parties have ever been ready to hurl this hideous weapon at those who have separated from them, from whatever cause; and the phrase has derived its chief power to injure from its vagueness. The Church of Rome has flung it at the Churches of the Reformation, and the Reformed Churches that stand at different degrees of distance from Rome, have been too ready to cast it at each other. Owen and his friends, now began to feel the injurious effects of this, in the frequent application of the term to themselves; and he was induced, in consequence, to write on the subject, with the view especially of distinguishing between the scriptural and the ecclesiastical use of the term, and, by simply defining it, to deprive it of its mischievous power. This led to his treatise, "Of Schism; the true nature of it discovered, and considered with reference to the present differences in region:" in which he shows that schism, as described in Scripture, consists in "causeless differences and contentions amongst the members of a particular church, contrary to that love, prudence, and forbearance, which are required of them to be exercised among themselves, and towards one another."[104] From this two consequences followed; — that separation from any church was

---

102 Preface to the reader.

103 Essay on the application of the epithet Romantic.

104 Owen's Works, xix. 132, 133, Russell's edition.

not in its own nature schism; and that those churches which, by their corruption or tyranny, rendered separation necessary, were the true schismatics: so that, as Vincent Alsop wittily remarked, "He that undertakes to play this great gun, had need to be very careful and spunge it well, lest it fire at home."[105] It is one of Dr Owen's best controversial treatises, being exhaustive, and yet not marked by that discursiveness which is the fault of some of his writings, and bringing into play some of his greatest excellencies as a writer, — his remarkable exegetical talent, his intimate knowledge of Scripture, and mastery of the stores of ecclesiastical history. Dr Hammond replied to him from among the Episcopalians, and Cawdrey from among the Presbyterians, — a stormy petrel, with whose spirit, Owen remarks, the Presbyterians in general had no sympathy; but Owen remained unquestionable master of the field.[106]

It was not thus with the controversy which we have next to describe. Owen had prepared a valuable little essay, — "Of the Divine Original, Authority, Self-evidencing Light and Power of the Scriptures; with an answer to that inquiry, How we know the Scriptures to be the word of God?" the principal design of which, as its title so far indicates, was to prove that, independently altogether of its external evidence, the Bible contains, in the nature of its truths and in their efficacy on the mind, sat-

---

105 Melius Inquirend., p. 209. Orme, p. 199. Wood's description of Alsop makes one suspect that he had smarted from his wit: "A Nonconforming minister, who, since the death of their famous A. Marvell, hath been quibbler and punner in ordinary to the Dissenting party, though he comes much short of that person." — Athen. Oxon., iv, 106.

106 The other writings drawn from Owen in this controversy were provoked by Cawdrey. — 1. A Review of the True Nature of Schism, with a Vindication of the Congregational Churches in England from the imputation thereof, unjustly charged on them by Mr Daniel Cawdrey, 1657. 2. An Answer to a late Treatise of Mr Cawdrey about the Nature of Schism, 1658, prefixed to a Defence of Mr John Cotton, &c., against Cawdrey, written by himself, and edited by Owen.

isfactory evidence of the divine source from which it has emanated; — an argument which was afterwards nobly handled by Halyburton, and which has recently been illustrated and illuminated by Dr Chalmers with his characteristic eloquence, in one of the chapters of his "Theological Institutes."[107] In this essay he had laid down the position, that "as the Scriptures of the Old and New Testament were immediately and entirely given out by God himself, — his mind being in them represented to us without the least interveniency of such mediums and ways as were capable of giving change or alteration to the least iota or syllable, — so, by his good and merciful providential dispensation, in his love to his Word and church, his Word as first given out by him is preserved unto us entire in the original languages."[108] It happened that while this essay was in the press, the Prolegomena and Appendix of Walton's invaluable and immortal work, the "London Polyglott," came into Owen's hands. But when he glanced at the formidable array of various readings, which was presented by Walton and his coadjutors as the result of their collation of manuscripts and versions, he became alarmed for his principles, imagined the authority of the Scriptures to be placed in imminent jeopardy, and, in an essay which he entitled, "A Vindication of the Purity and Integrity of the Hebrew and Greek Texts of the Old and New Testaments, in some considerations on the Prolegomena and Appendix to the late *Biblia Polyglotta*,"[109] rashly endeavoured to prove that Walton had greatly exaggerated the number of various readings, and insinuated his apprehension, that if Walton's principles were admitted, they would lead, by a very direct course, to Popery or Infidelity. It is needless to say how undeniable is the fact of various readings; how utterly groundless were the fears

---

107 Theological Institutes, x. b. iii. ch. 6.

108 P. 153, duod. ed.

109 Owen published a third tract in this little volume, "*Exercitations adversus Fanaticos*," in which he handled the Quakers with some severity.

which Dr Owen expressed because of them; and how much the labours of learned biblicists, in the region which was so nobly cultivated by Walton and his associates, have confirmed, instead of disturbing our confidence in the inspired canon.[110] And yet it is not difficult to understand how the same individual, who was unsurpassed, perhaps unequalled, in his own age in his knowledge of the subject-matter of revelation, should have been comparatively uninformed on questions which related to the integrity of the sacred text itself. The error of Owen consisted in making broad assertions on a subject on which he acknowledged himself to be, after all, but imperfectly informed; and, from a mere *a priori* ground, challenging facts that were sustained by very abundant evidence, and charging those facts with the most revolting consequences. Let those theologians be warned by it, who, on the ground of preconceived notions and incorrect interpretations of Scripture, have called in question some of the plainest discoveries of science; and be assured that truth, come from what quarter it may, can never place the Word of God in jeopardy.

Walton saw that he had the advantage of Owen, and in "The Considerator Considered, and the *Biblia Polyglotta* Vindicated," successfully defended his position, and did what he could to hold Owen up to the ridicule of the learned world. Though he was Owen's victor in this controversy, yet the arrogance of his bearing excites the suspicion that something more than learned zeal bore him into the contest, and that the exasperated feelings of the ecclesiastic made him not unwilling to humble this leader and champion of the Puritans in the dust. The respective merits of the two combatants in this contest, which excited so much commotion in the age in which it occurred, are admirably remarked on by Dr Chalmers: "The most interesting collision upon this question that I know of, between unlike men of unlike minds, was that between the most learned of our Churchmen

---

110 Marsh's Michaelis, i. ch. vi. Taylor's History of the Transmission of Ancient Books; appendix.

on the one hand, Brian Walton, author, or rather editor of the 'London Polyglott,' and the most talented and zealous of our sectarians on the other, Dr John Owen. The latter adventured himself most rashly into a combat, and under a false alarm for the results of the erudition of the former; and the former retorted contemptuously upon his antagonist, as he would upon a mystic or enthusiastic devotee. The amalgamation of the two properties thus arrayed in hostile conflict, would have just made up a perfect theologian. It would have been the wisdom of the letter in alliance with the wisdom of the spirit; instead of which I know not what was most revolting, — the lordly insolence of the prelate, or the outrageous violence of the Puritan. In the first place, it was illiterate in Owen, to apprehend that the integrity of the Scripture would be unsettled by the exposure, in all their magnitude and multitude, of its various readings; but in the second place, we stand in doubt of Walton's spirit and his seriousness, when he groups and characterizes as the new-light men and ranting enthusiasts of these days, those sectaries, many of whom, though far behind him in the lore of theology as consisting in the knowledge of its vocables, were as far before him in acquaintance with the subject-matter of theology, as consisting of its doctrines, and of their application to the wants and the principles of our moral nature."[111]

About the time of his emerging from this unfortunate controversy, Owen gave to the world his work on Temptation, — another of those masterly treatises in which he "brings the doctrines of theology to bear on the wants and principles of our moral nature," and from which whole paragraphs flash upon the mind of the reader with an influence that makes him feel as if they had been written for himself alone.

In his preface to that work, Owen (no doubt reflecting his impressions of public events) speaks of "providential dispensations, in reference to the public concernments of these nations, as perplexed and entangled, — the footsteps of God lying in the

---

111 Institutes of Theology, i. 287 — On Scripture Criticism.

deep, where his paths are not known." And certainly the rapid and turbulent succession of changes that took place soon after the removal of Cromwell's presiding genius from the helm, might well fill him with deepening anxiety and alarm. These changes it is not our province minutely to trace. Richard's feeble hand, as is well known, proved itself unfit to control the opposing elements of the state; and a few months saw him return not unwillingly, to the unambitious walks of private life.[112] Owen has been charged with talking part in the schemes which drove Richard from the Protectorate; but the charge proceeded upon a mere impression of Dr Manton's, produced from hearing the fragment of a conversation, and was repeatedly and indignantly denied by Owen during his life.[113] Then followed the recalling of that remnant of the Long Parliament which had been dispersed by Cromwell, — a measure which Owen advised, as, on the whole, the most likely to secure the continuance of an unrestricted liberty. But the Parliament, unwilling to obey the dictation of a dominant party in the Army, was once more dispersed by force, while the army itself began to be divided into ambitious factions. A new danger threatened from the north. General Monk, marking the state of things in England, and especially the divided condition of the army, was making prepa-

---

112 Owen's sermon, "A Gospel Profession, the Glory of a Nation," Isa. iv. 5, was preached before Richard's Parliament. Soon after, he preached before the Long Parliament; and this was the last occasion in which he was invited to officiate before such an assemblage. This sermon has not been preserved.

113 Dr Manton declared, that at Wallingford House he heard Dr Owen say with vehemence, "He must come down, and he shall come down;" and this was understood to refer to Richard; — but it is material to notice that Dr Manton did not so understand it till after the event. — Palmer's note to Calamy's Life of Owen. Noncon. Mem., i. 201. Add to this Owen's solemn denial of the charge, Vindic. of Animadversions on *Fiat Lux*, p. 127; and the testimony of a "worthy minister," preserved by Asty, that Dr Owen was against the pulling down of Richard, and this his dissatisfaction at what they were doing at Wallingford House was such as to drive his into illness. — Asty, p. xix.

IV. His Retirement and Last Days

rations to enter England. What were his designs? At one period he had befriended the Independents, but latterly he had sided with the powerful body of the Presbyterians. Would he now, then, endeavour to set up a new Protectorate, favouring the Presbyterians and oppressing other sects or would he throw his sword into the scale of the Royalists, and bring back the Stuarts? A deputation of Independent ministers, consisting of Caryl and others, was sent into Scotland, bearing a letter to Monk that had been written by Owen, representing to him the injustice of his entering England, and the danger to which it would expose their most precious liberties. But the deputies returned, unable to influence his movements, or even to penetrate his ultimate designs. Owen and his friends next endeavoured to arouse the army to a vigorous resistance of Monk, and even offered to raise £100,000 among the Independents for their assistance; — but they found the army divided and dispirited; and Monk, gradually approaching London, entered it at length, not only unresisted, but welcomed by thousands, the Long Parliament having again found courage to resume its sittings. In a short while the Long Parliament was finally dissolved by its own content, and soon after the Convention Parliament assembled. Monk at length threw off his hitherto impenetrable disguise, and ventured to introduce letters from Charles Stuart. It was voted, at his instigation, that the ancient constitution of King, Lords, and Commons, should be restored, and Charles invited back to the throne of his ancestors; and the great majority of the nation, weary of the years of faction and turbulence, hailed the change with joy. But in the enthusiasm of the moment, no means were taken to secure an adjustment of those vital questions which had been agitated between the people and the crown. The act, therefore, which restored the king, restored the laws, both civil and ecclesiastical, to the state in which they had been at the commencement of the war, re-established the hierarchy, and constituted all classes of separatists a proscribed class; and Owen and his party had little to trust to for the continuance of their religious liberties but the promise of Charles at Breda, that he "would have a respect to tender consciences."[114] A little time sufficed to show that the king's word was but a miserable security; and the beautiful words of Baxter now began to be fulfilled in their darkest part: "Ordinarily, God would have vicissitudes of summer and winter, day and night, that the church may grow externally in the summer of prosperity, and internally and radically in the winter of adversity; yet usually their night is longer than their day, and that day itself has its storms and tempests." The night was now coming to the Puritans.

A few months before the restoration of Charles, Owen had been displaced from the deanery of Christ Church, and thus his last official connection with Oxford severed. He now retired to his native village of Stadham in the neighbourhood, where he had become the proprietor of a small estate. During his vice-chancellorship, it had been his custom to preach in this place on the afternoons of those Sabbaths in which he was not employed at St. Mary's; and a little congregation which he had gathered by this means now joyfully welcomed him among them as their pastor. It was probably while at Stadham that he finished the preparation of one of his most elaborate theological works, whose title will supply a pretty accurate idea at once of its general plan and of its remarkable variety of matter, — "Theologoumena, etc.; or, six books on the nature, rise, progress, and study of true theology. In which, also, the origin and growth of true and false religious worship, and the more remarkable declensions and restorations of the church are traced from their first sources. To which are added digressions concerning universal grace, — the origin of the sciences, — notes of the Roman Church, — the origin of letters, — the ancient Hebrew letters, — Hebrew punctuation, — versions of the Scriptures, — Jewish rites," etc. It is matter of regret that the "Theologoumena" has hitherto been locked up in the Latin tongue; for though parts have been superseded by more recent

---

114 Neal, iv. 191–220. Vaughan's Stuart Dynasty, ii. 266–271.

IV. His Retirement and Last Days

works, there is no book in the English language that occupies the wide field over which Owen travels with his usual power, and scatters around him his learned stores.[115]

In all likelihood Owen hoped that he would be permitted to remain unmolested in his quiet village, and that his very obscurity would prove his protection; but he had miscalculated the leniency of the new rulers. An act passed against the Quakers, declared it illegal for more than five persons to assemble in any unauthorized place for religious worship; and this act admitting of application to all separatists, soon led to the expulsion of Owen from his charge, and to the dispersion of his little flock.[116] In a little while he saw himself surrounded by many companions in tribulation. The Presbyterians, who had shown such eagerness for the restoration of Charles to his throne, naturally expected that such measures would be taken as would comprehend them within the establishment, without doing violence to their conscientious difficulties; and Charles and his ministers flattered the hope so long as they thought it unsafe to despise it; but it was not long ere the Act of Uniformity drove nearly two thousand of them from their churches into persecution and poverty, and brought once more into closer fellowship with Owen those excellent men whom he had continued to love and esteem in the midst of all their mutual differences.

Sir Edward Hyde, the future Lord Clarendon, was now lord chancellor, and the most influential member of the government, and means were used to obtain an interview between Owen and him, with the view, it is probable, of inducing him to relax the growing severity of his measures against the Nonconformists. But the proud minister was inexorable. He insisted that Owen should abstain from preaching; but at the one time, not ignorant of the great talents of the Puritan, strongly urged him to em-

---

115 A portion of the "Theologoumena" was translated and published by the Rev. J. Craig of Avonbridge in Scotland; but the encouragement was not such as to induce him to persevere.

116 Wood's Athen. Oxon., iv. 100.

ploy his pen at the present juncture in writing against Popery. Owen did not comply with the first part of the injunction, but continued to preach in London and elsewhere, to little secret assemblies, and even at times more publicly, when the vigilance of informers was relaxed, or the winds of persecution blew for a little moment less fiercely. But circumstances soon put it in his power to comply with the latter part of it; and those circumstances are interesting, both as illustrative of the character of Owen and of the spirit and tendencies of the times.

John Vincent Cane, a Franciscan friar, had published a book entitled, "*Fiat Lux*; or, a Guide in Differences of Religion betwixt Papist and Protestant, Presbyterian and Independent;" in which, under the guise of recommending moderation and charity, he invites men over to the Church of Rome, as the only infallible remedy for all church divisions. The work falling in to some extent with the current of feeling in certain quarters, had already gone through two impressions ere it reached the hands of Owen, and is believed to have been sent to him at length by Clarendon. Struck with the subtle and pernicious character of the work, whose author he describes as "a Naphtali speaking goodly words, but while his voice was Jacob's voice, his hands were the hands of Esau," Owen set himself to answer it, and soon produced his "Animadversions on *Fiat Lux*, by a Protestant;" which so completely exposed its sophistries and hidden aims, as to make the disconcerted friar lose his temper. The friar replied in a "Vindication of *Fiat Lux*," — in which he betrayed a vindictive wish to detect his opponent, and bring upon him the resentment of those in power; describing him as "a part of that dismal tempest which had borne all before it, — not only church and state, but reason, right, honesty, and all true religion."[117] To which Owen rejoined, now manfully giving his name, and, according to his custom, not satisfied with answering his immediate opponent, entered largely into the whole Popish controversy. Few things are more remarkable in Owen than the readiness

---

117 Vindic. of Animad. on *Fiat Lux*, p. 10.

IV. His Retirement and Last Days

with which he could thus summon to his use the vast stores of his accumulated learning.

But, even after this good service had been done to the common cause of Protestantism, there seemed a danger that this second work would not be permitted to be published; and it is curious to notice the nature of the objections, and the quarter whence they came. The power of licensing books in divinity was now in the hands of the bishops; and they were found to have two weighty objections to Owen's treatise. First, That in speaking of the evangelists and apostles, and even of Peter, he withheld from them the title of "saint;" and, secondly, That he had questioned whether it could be proved that Peter had ever been at Rome. Owen's treatment of these objections was every way worthy of himself. In reference to the former, he reminded his censors that the titles of evangelist and apostle were superior to that of saint, inasmuch as this belonged to all the people of God; at the same time, he expressed his willingness to yield this point. But the second he could only yield on one condition, — namely, that they would prove that he had been mistaken. Owen's book at length found its way to the press; not, however, through the concessions of the bishops, but through the command of Sir Edward Nicolas, one of the principal secretaries of state, who interposed to overrule their scruples.[118]

Dr Owen's reputation was greatly extended by these writings; and this led to a new interview with Clarendon. His lordship acknowledged that he had done more for the cause of Protestantism than any other man in England; and, expressing his astonishment that so learned a man should have been led away by "the novelty of Independency," held out to him the hope of high preferment in the church if he would conform. Owen undertook to prove, in answer to any bishop that he might appoint, that the Independent form of church order, instead of being a novelty, was the only mode of government in the church for the first two centuries; and as for his wish to bestow upon

---

118 Asty, pp. xxiii., xxiv.

him ecclesiastical honours, what he had to ask for himself and his brethren was, not preferment within the church, but simple toleration without it. The dazzling bait of a mitre appears to have been set before all the leading Nonconformists; but not one of them yielded to its lure.[119] This led the chancellor to inquire what was the measure of toleration he had to ask; — to which Owen is reported to have answered, "Liberty for all who assented to the doctrine of the Church of England." This answer has been remarked on by some at the expense of his consistency and courage; and the explanation has been suggested, that he now asked not all that he wished, but all that there was the most distant hope of receiving. It should be remembered, however, in addition, that many of the most liberal and enlightened men among the Nonconformists of those days objected to the full toleration of Papists;[120] not, indeed, on religious, but on political grounds; — both because they were the subjects of a foreign power, and because of the bearings of the question on the succession of the Duke of York to the throne; and also, that Owen's plan would actually have comprehended in it almost the whole of the Protestant Nonconformists of that age.

A more honourable way of deliverance from his troubles than conformity was, about the same time, presented to Dr Owen, in an earnest invitation from the first Congregational church of Boston, in New England, to become their pastor. They had "seen his labours, and heard of the grace and wisdom communicated to him from the Father of lights;" and when so many candles were not permitted to shine in England, they were eager to secure such a burning light for their infant colony. It does not very clearly appear what sort of answer Owen returned. One biographer represents him as willing to go, and as even hav-

---

119 "I am informed," says the author of the Anonymous Memoir, "by one of the Doctor's relations, that King Charles II. offered him a bishopric; but no worldly honour or advantage could prevail upon the Doctor to change his principles." — P. xxii.

120 Owen's Discourse of Toleration, *passim*.

ing some of his property embarked in a vessel bound for New England, when he was stopped by orders of the court; others represent him as unwilling to leave behind him the struggling cause, and disposed to wait in England for happier days.[121]

But neither the representations of Owen nor of others who were friendly to the Nonconformists, had any influence in changing the policy of those who were now in power. The golden age to which Clarendon and his associates sought to bring back the government and the country, was that of Laud, with all the tortures of the Star Chamber, the dark machinery of the High Commission, and the dread alternative of abject conformity, or proscription and ruin. And the licentious Charles, while affecting at times a greater liberality, joined with his ministers in their worst measures; either from a secret sympathy with them, or, as is more probable, from a hope that the ranks of Nonconformity would at length be so greatly swelled as to render a measure of toleration necessary that would include in it the Romanist along with the Puritan. Pretexts were sought after and eagerly seized upon, in order to increase the rigours of persecution; and new acts passed, such as the Conventicle Act, which declared it penal to hold meetings for worship, even in barns and highways, and offered high rewards to informers, — and whose deliberate intention was, either to compel the sufferers to conformity, or to goad them on to violence and crime.

In the midst of these growing rigours, which were rapidly filling the prisons with victims, and crowding the emigrant ships with exiles, the plague appeared, sweeping London as with a whirlwind of death. Then it was seen who had been the true spiritual shepherds of the people, and who had been the strangers and the hirelings. The clerical oppressors of the Puritans fled from the presence of the plague, while the proscribed preachers emerged from their hiding-places, shared the dangers

---

121 Anthony Wood is amusingly cynical in his account of this matter: "Upon this our author resolved to go to New England; but since that time, the wind was never in a right point for a voyage." — Wood's Athen. Oxon., iv. 100.

of that dreadful hour, addressed instruction and consolation to the perishing and bereaved, and stood between the living and the dead, until the plague was stayed. One thing, however, had been disclosed by these occurrences; and this was the undiminished influence of the Nonconformist pastors over their people, and the increased love of their people to them; nor could the pastors ever be cut off from the means of temporal support, so long as intercourse between them and their people was maintained. This led to the passing of another act, whose ingenious cruelty historians have vied with each other adequately to describe. In the Parliament at Oxford, which had fled thither in order to escape the ravages of the plague, a law was enacted which virtually banished all Nonconformist ministers five miles from any city, town, or borough, that sent members to Parliament, and five miles from any place whatsoever where they had at any time in a number of years past preached; unless they would take an oath which it was well-known no Nonconformist could take, and which the Earl of Southampton even declared, in his place in Parliament, no honest man could subscribe. This was equivalent to driving them into exile in their own land; and, in addition to the universal severance of the pastors from their people, by banishing them into remote rural districts, it exposed them not only to the caprice of those who were the instruments of government, and to all the vile acts of spies and informers, but often to the insults and the violence of ignorant and licentious mobs.

Dr Owen suffered in the midst of all these troubles; and one anecdote, which most probably belongs to this period, presents us with another picture of the times. He had gone down to visit his old friends in the neighbourhood of Oxford, and adopting the usual precautions of the period, had approached his lodging after nightfall. But notwithstanding all his privacy, he was observed, and information given of the place where he lay. Early in the morning, a company of troopers came and knocked at the door. The mistress coming down, boldly opened the door, and asked them what they would have. — "Have you any lodgers in your house?" they inquired. Instead of directly answering their question, she asked "whether they were seeking for Dr Owen?" "Yes," said they; on which she assured them he had departed that morning at an earlier hour. The soldiers believing her word, immediately rode away. In the meantime the Doctor, whom the woman really supposed to have been gone, as he intended the night before, arose, and going into a neighbouring field, whither he ordered his horse to be brought to him, hastened away by an unfrequented path towards London.

A second terrible visitation of Heaven was needed, in order to obtain for the persecuted Puritans a temporary breathing-time: and this second visitation came. The fire followed quickly in the footsteps of the plague, and the hand of intolerance was for the moment paralysed, if, indeed, its heart did not for a time relent. The greater number of the churches were consumed in the dreadful conflagration. Large wooden houses called tabernacles were quickly reared, amid the scorched and blackened ruins; and in these, the Nonconformist ministers preached to anxious and solemnized multitudes. The long silent voices of Owen, and Manton, and Caryl, and others, awoke the remembrance of other times; and earnest Baxter

> "Preached as though he never should preach again;
> And like a dying man to dying men."

There was no possibility of silencing these preachers at such a moment. And the fall of Clarendon and the disgrace of Sheldon soon afterwards helped to prolong and enlarge their precarious liberty.

Many tracts, for the most part published anonymously, and without even the printer's name, had issued from Owen's pen during these distracting years, having for their object to represent the impolicy and injustice of persecution for conscience' sake.[122] He had also published "A Brief Instruction in

---

122 Of these Mr Orme enumerates the following:— 1. "An Account of the Grounds and Reasons on which the Protestant Dissenters

the Worship of God and Discipline of the Churches of the New Testament, by way of question and answer," — a title which sufficiently describes the book;[123] and some years earlier, a well compacted and admirably reasoned "Discourse concerning Liturgies and their Imposition," which illustrates the principle on which, when a student at Oxford, he had resisted the impositions of Laud, — a principle which reaches to the very foundation of the argument between the High Churchman and the Puritan. And his publications during the following year show with what untiring assiduity, in the midst of all those outward storms, he had been plying the work of authorship, and laying up rich stores for posterity. Three of Owen's best works bear the date of 1668.

First, there is his treatise "On the Nature, Power, Deceit, and Prevalence of Indwelling Sin in Believers;" on which Dr Chalmers has well remarked, that "there is no treatise of its learned and pious author more fitted to be useful to the Christian disciple; and that it is most important to be instructed on this subject by one who had reached such lofty attainments in holiness, and whose profound and experimental acquaintance with the spiritual life so well fitted him for expounding its nature and operations."[124] Next came his "Exposition of the 130th Psalm," — a work which, as we have already hinted, stood in-

---

Desire their Liberty." 2. "A Letter concerning the Present Excommunications." 3. "The Present Distresses on Nonconformists Examined." 4. "Indulgence and Toleration Considered, in a Letter to a Person of Honour." 5. "A Peace-offering, in an Apology and Humble Plea for Liberty of Conscience." — P. 234.

123 The publication of this Catechism gave occasion to proposals for union among the Presbyterians and Independents, addressed by the sanguine Baxter to Dr Owen, and led to lengthened correspondence and negotiation. For reasons formerly adverted to, the scheme proved abortive. One of Owen's letters on this subject has been preserved, and appears in the Appendix. We are not sure that in every part we could vindicate the Doctor's consistency.

124 Introductory Essay to Owen on Indwelling Sin, pp. xviii., xix.

timately connected with the history of Owen's own inner life; and which, conducting the reader through the turnings and windings along many of which he himself had wandered in the season of his spiritual distresses, shows him the way in which he at length found peace. When Owen sat down to the exposition of this psalm, it was not with the mere literary implements of study scattered around him, or in the spirit with which the mere scholar may be supposed to sit down to the explanation of an ancient classic; but, when he laid open the book of God, he laid open at the same time the book of his own heart and of his own history, and produced a book which, with all its acknowledged prolixity, and even its occasional obscurity, is rich in golden thoughts, and instinct with the living experience of "one who spoke what he knew, and testified what he had seen."

Then appeared the first volume of Owen's greatest work, his "Exposition of the Epistle to the Hebrews," — a work which it would be alike superfluous to describe or to praise.[125] For more than twenty years his thoughts had been turned to the preparing of this colossal commentary on the most difficult of all the Pauline epistles; and at length he had given himself to it with ripened powers, — with the gathered treasures of an almost universal reading, and with the richer treasures still of a deep Christian experience. Not disdainful of the labours of those who had gone before him, he yet found that the mine had been opened, rather than exhausted; and, as he himself strongly expressed it, that "sufficient ground for renewed investigation had been left, not only for the present generation, but for all them that should succeed, to the consummation of all things." The spirit and manner in which he pursued his work is described by himself, and forms one of the most valuable portions of autobiography in all Owen's writings: —

"For the exposition of the epistle itself, I confess, as was said

---

[125] The second volume was published in 1674; the third in 1680; the forth was posthumous, but was left fit for the press, and appeared in 1684.

before, that I have had thoughts of it for many years, and have not been without regard to it in the whole course of my studies. But yet I must now say, that, after all my searching and reading, prayer and assiduous meditation have been my only resort, and by far the most useful means of light and assistance. By these have my thought been freed from many an entanglement, into which the writings of others had cast me, or from which they could not deliver me. Careful I have been, as of my life and soul, to bring no prejudicate sense to the words, — to impose no meaning of my own or other men's upon them, nor to be imposed on by the reasonings, pretences, or curiosities of any; but always went nakedly to the Word itself, to learn humbly the mind of God in it, and to express it as he should enable me. To this end, I always considered, in the first place, the sense, meaning, and import of the words of the text, — their original derivation, use in other authors, especially in the LXX. of the Old Testament, in the books of the New, and particularly the writings of the same author. Ofttimes the words expressed out of the Hebrew, or the things alluded to among that people, I found to give much light to the words of the apostle. To the general rule of attending to the design and scope of the place, the subject treated of, mediums fixed on for arguments, and methods of reasoning, I still kept in my eye the time and season of writing this epistle; the state and condition of those to whom it was written; their persuasions, prejudices, customs, light, and traditions. I kept also in my view the covenant and worship of the church of old; the translation of covenant privileges and worship to the Gentiles upon a new account; the course of providential dispensations that the Jews were under; the near expiration of their church and state; the speedy approach of their utter abolition and destruction, with the temptations that befell them on all these various accounts; — without which it is impossible for any one justly to follow the apostle, so as to keep close to his design or fully to understand his meaning."[126]

---

126 Preface.

IV. His Retirement and Last Days

The result has been, a work unequalled in excellence, except, perhaps, by Vitringa's noble commentary on Isaiah. It is quite true, that in the department of verbal criticism, and even in the exposition of some occasional passages, future expositors may have found Owen at fault, — it is even true that the Rabbinical lore with which the work abounds does far more to cumber than to illustrate the text; but when all this has been conceded, how amazing is the power with which Owen has unfolded the proportions, and brought out the meaning and spirit, of this massive epistle! It is like some vast monster filled with solemn light, on whose minuter details it might be easy to suggest improvement; but whose stable walls and noble columns astonish you at the skill and strength of the builder the longer you gaze; and there is true sublimity in the exclamation with which Owen laid down his pen when he had finished it: "Now, my work is done; it is time for me to die." Perhaps no minister in Great Britain or America for the last hundred and fifty years has sat down to the exposition of this portion of inspired truth without consulting Owen's commentary. The appalling magnitude of the work is the most formidable obstacle to its usefulness; and this the author himself seems to have anticipated even in his own age of ponderous and portly folios; for we find him modestly suggesting the possibility of treating it as if it were three separate works, and of reading the philological, or the exegetical, or the practical portion alone.[127] We are quite aware that one man of great eminence has spoken in terms of disparagement almost bordering on contempt of one part of this great work, — "The Preliminary Exercitations;"[128] but we must remember Hall's love of literary paradoxes, in common with the great lexicographer whom he imitated; and those who are familiar with the writings of Owen — which Hall acknowledges he was not,

---

127 Address to the Christian Reader, vol. ii.

128 Miscellaneous Gleanings from Hall's Conversational Remarks, by the late Dr Balmer of Berwick-on-Tweed. Hall's Works, vi. 147.

— will be more disposed to subscribe to the glowing terms in which his great rival in eloquence has spoken of Owen's Exposition: "Let me again recommend your studious and sustained attention," says Dr Chalmers to his students, "to the Epistle to the Hebrews; and I should rejoice if any of you felt emboldened on my advice to grapple with a work so ponderous as Owen's commentary on that epistle, — a lengthened and laborious enterprise, certainly, but now is your season for abundant labour. And the only thing to be attended to is, that, in virtue of being well directed, it shall not be wasted on a bulky, though at the same time profitless erudition. I promise you a hundredfold more advantage from the perusal of this greatest work of John Owen, than from the perusal of all that has been written on the subject of the heathen sacrifices. It is a work of gigantic strength as well as gigantic size; and he who has mastered it is very little short, both in respect to the doctrinal and the practical of Christianity, of being an erudite and accomplished theologian."[129]

It has been remarked, that there is no lesson so difficult to learn as that of true religious toleration, for almost every sect in turn, when tempted by the power, has resorted to the practice of persecution; and this remark has seldom obtained more striking confirmation than in what was occurring at this time in another part of the world. While in England the Independents, and Nonconformists generally, were passing from one degree of persecution to another, at the hands of the restored adherents of Prelacy; the Independents of New England were perpetrating even greater severities against the Baptists and Quakers in that infant colony. Whipping, fines, imprisonment, selling into slavery, were punishments inflicted by them on thousands who, after all, did not differ from their persecutors on any point that was fundamental in religion. One of Owen's biographers has taken very unnecessary pains to show that the conduct of these churches had no connection with their principles as Inde-

---

129 Prelections on Hill's lectures. Chalmer's Posthumous Works, ix. 282.

pendents; but this only renders their conduct the more inexcusable, and proves how deeply rooted the spirit of intolerance is in human nature. Owen and his friends heard of these events with indignation and shame, and even feared that they might be turned to their disadvantage in England; and, in a letter subscribed along with him by all his brethren in London, faithfully remonstrated with the New England persecutors. "We only make it our hearty request," said they, "that you will trust God with his truth and ways, so far as to suspend all rigorous proceedings in corporeal restraints or punishments on persons that dissent from you, and practice the principles of their dissent without danger or disturbance to the civil peace of the place." Sound advice is here given, but we should have relished a little more of the severity of stern rebuke.[130]

We have seen that the great fire of London led to a temporary connivance at the public preaching of the Nonconformist ministers; "it being at the first," as Baxter remarked, "too gross to forbid an undone people all public worship with too great rigour."[131] A scheme was soon after devised for giving to this liberty a legal sanction, and which might even perhaps incorporate many of the Nonconformists with the Established Church, — such men as Wilkins, bishop of Chester, Tillotson, and Stillingfleet, warmly espousing the proposal. But no sooner did the scheme become generally known, as well as the influential names by which it was approved, than the implacable adversaries of the Nonconformists anew bestirred themselves, and succeeded in extinguishing its generous provisions. It became necessary, however, in the temper of the nation, to do something in vindication of these severities; and no readier expedient suggested itself than to decry toleration as unfriendly to social order, and still more to blacken the character of the Nonconformist sufferers. A fit instrument for this work presented

---

130 M'Crie's Miscellaneous Works, p. 509. *Magnalia Americana*, b. vii. p. 28. Orme p. 258.

131 Own Life, part iii. p. 20.

himself in Samuel Parker, a man of menial origin, who had for a time been connected with the Puritans, but who, deserting them when they became sufferers, was now aspiring after preferment in the Episcopal Church, and whom Burnet describes as "full of satirical vivacity, considerably learned, but of no judgment; and as to religion, rather impious."[132] In his "Discourse of Ecclesiastical Polity," the "authority of the civil magistrate over the consciences of subjects in matters of external religion is asserted, the mischief and inconveniences of toleration are represented, and all pretences pleaded in favour of liberty of conscience are fully answered." Such is the atrocious title-page of his book, and to a modern reader, the undertaking to which it pledges him must seem rather bold; but the confident author is reported to have firmly believed in his own success. Holding out his book to the Earl of Anglesea, he said, "Let us see, my lord, whether any of your chaplains can answer it;" and the bigoted Sheldon, sympathizing with its spirit, naturally believed also in the exceeding force of its arguments. Dr Owen was chosen to reply to Parker; which he did, in one of the noblest controversial treatises that were ever penned by him, — "Truth and Innocence Vindicated, in a Survey of a Discourse on Ecclesiastical Polity," etc. The mind of Owen seems to have been whetted by his deep sense of wrong, and he writes with a remarkable clearness and force of argument; while he indulges at times in a style of irony which is justified not more by the folly than by the baseness and wickedness of Parker's sentiments. There is no passage, even in the writings of Locke, in which the province of the civil magistrate is more distinctly defined than in some portions of his reply;[133] and it is curious to notice how, in his allusions to trade, he anticipates some of the most established principles of our modern political economy.[134] Owen's work greatly increased his

---

132 Burnet's Own Times, i. 382.

133 Duod. ed., p. 92.

134 Duod. ed., pp. 78–81.

IV. His Retirement and Last Days

celebrity among his brethren; — even some of Parker's friends could with difficulty conceal the impression that he had found more than a match in the strong-minded and sturdy Puritan; and Parker, worsted in argument, next sought to overwhelm his opponent with a scurrility that breathed the most undisguised vindictiveness. He was "the great bell-wether of disturbance and sedition," — "a person who would have vied with Mahomet himself both for boldness and imposture," — "a viper, so swollen with venom that it must either burst or spit its poison;" so that whoever wished to do well to his country, "could never do it better service than by beating down the interest and reputation of such sons of Belial."[135] On this principle, at least, Parker himself might have ranked high as a patriot.

But the controversy was not over. Parker had not time to recover from the ponderous club of Owen, when he was assailed by the keen edged wit of Andrew Marvell. This accomplished man, the under-secretary and bosom friend of Milton, reviewed Parker's work in his "Rehearsal Transposed," — a work of which critics have spoken as rivalling in some places the causticity and neatness of Swift, and in others equalling the eloquent invective of Junius and the playful exuberance of Burke.[136] The conceited ecclesiastic was overwhelmed, and a number of masked combatants perceiving his plight, now rushed to his defence; in all whom, however, Marvell refused to distinguish any but Parker. In a second part of his "Rehearsal," he returned to the pen-combat, as Wood has called it; and transfixed his victim with new arrows from his exhaustless quiver. It is impossible to read many parts of it yet, without sharing with the laughers of the age in the influence of Marvell's genius. Ridiculing his self-importance, he says, "If he chance but to sneeze, he prays that *the foundations of the earth be not shaken.* Ever since he crept

---

135 Defence and Continuation of Eccleisast. Polity, and Preface to Bamhall. Orme, p. 261.

136 Campbell's Essay on English Poetry, p. 241. D'Israeli's Miscellanies of Literature, p. 238.

up to be but *the weather-cock of a steeple*, he trembles and cracks at every puff of wind that blows about him, as *if the Church of England were falling*." Marvell's wit was triumphant; and even Charles and his court joined in laughing at Parker's discomfiture.[137] "Though the delinquent did not lay violent hands on himself," says D'Israeli, "he did what, for an author, may be considered as desperate a course, — withdraw from the town, and cease writing for many years," secretly nursing a revenge which he did not dare to gratify until he knew that Marvell was in his grave.[138]

It was one thing, however, to conquer in the field of argument, and another thing to disarm the intolerance of those in power. The Parliament which met in 1671, goaded on by those sleepless ecclesiastics who were animated by the malign spirit of Parker, confirmed all the old acts against the Nonconformists, and even passed others of yet more intolerable rigour.[139] It is impossible to predict to what consequences the enforcement of these measures must soon have led, had not Charles, by his declaration of indulgence, of his own authority suspended the penal statutes against Nonconformists and Popish recusants, and given them permission to renew their meetings for public worship on their procuring a license, which would be granted for that purpose. This measure was, no doubt, unconstitutional in its form, and more than doubtful in the motives which prompted it; but many of the Nonconformists, seeing in it only the restoration of a right of which they ought never to have

---

[137] Burnet, referring to this controversy, speaks of Marvell as "the liveliest droll of his age, who writ in a burlesque strain, but with so peculiar and so entertaining a conduct, that, from the king down to the tradesman, his books were read with great pleasure." — Own Times, i. 382.

[138] D'Israeli's Miscellanies, pp. 234, 239.

[139] A paper entitled, "The State of the Kingdom with respect to the present Bill against Conventicles," was drawn up by Owen, and laid before the Lords by several eminent citizens; but without success.

been deprived, — and some of them, like Owen, regarding it as "an expedient, according to the custom in former times, for the peace and security of the kingdom, until the whole matter might be settled in Parliament," joyfully took shelter under its provisions.[140]

The Nonconformists were prompt in improving their precarious breathing-time. A weekly lecture was instituted at Pinner's Hall by the Presbyterians and Independents, in testimony of their union of sentiment on fundamental truths, and as an antidote to Popish, Socinian, and Infidel opinions.[141] Owen began to preach more publicly in London to a regular congregation; and his venerable friend, Joseph Caryl, having died soon after the declaration of indulgence, the congregations of the two ministers consented to unite under the ministry of Owen, in the place of worship in Leadenhall Street.[142] Owen's church-book presents the names of some of the chiefs of Nonconformity as members of his flock, and "honourable women not a few."[143] Among others, there have been found the names of more than one of the heroes of the army of the Commonwealth, — such

---

140 Biographers make mention of letters addressed to Owen, inviting him to the presidency of Harvard College, New England; and also to a professorship in the United Provinces. But there is considerable vagueness in respect to details, as well as uncertainty about dates. A note, however, in Wood's Athen. Oxon., seems to place beyond reasonable doubt the general accuracy of the statement. He is said by the same authority to have been prevented from accepting the former invitation by an order from court.

141 Two lectures preached by Owen in this series appear among his works, — the first entitled, "How we may Learn to Bear Reproofs," Ps. cxli. 5; the other, "The Chamber of Imagery in the Church of Rome Laid Open," 1 Pet. ii. 3.

142 Mr Orme supposes the place of worship to have been that in Bury Street, St Mary Axe; but the meeting-house was in Bury Street was not erected until 1708, when it was occupied by the same congregation under the ministry of Dr Isaac Watts. — Wilson's History of Dissenting Churches, i. 252, 273.

143 Orme, pp. 277–285.

as Lord Charles Fleetwood and Colonel Desborough; certain members of the Abney family, in whose hospitable mansion the saintly Isaac Watts in after times found shelter for more than thirty years; the Countess of Anglesea; and Mrs Bendish, the grand-daughter of Cromwell, in whom, it is said, may of the bodily and mental features of the Protector remarkably reappeared. Some of these might be able at times to throw their shield over the head of Owen in those changeful and stormy years. And there were other persons more powerful still, — such as the Earl of Orrery, the Earl of Anglesea, Lord Berkeley, Lord Willoughby, Lord Wharton, and Sir John Trevor, one of the principal secretaries of state; who, though not members of Owen's church, were religiously disposed, and Owen's friends, and inclined, as far as their influence went, to mitigate the severities against the Nonconformists generally.[144]

Owen's intimacy with these noblemen probably accounts for that interview to which he was invited by the King and the Duke of York, and which has been faithfully chronicled by all his biographers. Happening to be at Tunbridge Wells when his majesty and the duke were also there, he was introduced to the royal tent. The king freely conversed with him on the subject of religious liberty, and expressed his wish to see the Dissenters relieved of their disabilities. On his return to London, he invited Owen to repeated interviews, uttering the same sentiments as he had done during the first conversation, and at length intrusted him with a thousand guineas, to be employed by him in mitigating the sufferings of his poorer brethren. The general policy of Charles sufficiently accounts for these gleams of royal sunshine.

But the importance of those friendships is not seen by us until we have marked the use which Owen made of them in the cause of his suffering brethren. It is well known that when the Parliament again assembled, it expressed its strong displeasure at the king's indulgence, and never ceased its remonstrances

---

144 Asty, p. xxix. Noncon. Mem., i. 202.

IV. His Retirement and Last Days

until the licenses to places of worship had been withdrawn. A disposition, it is true, began to show itself to distinguish between the Protestant Nonconformists and the Romanists, and to point restriction more particularly against the latter; but the act, which was professedly intended to bear against *them* was so clumsily constructed as to be capable of reaching all who did not conform, and Churchmen were not slow in giving it this direction. The Nonconformists were exposed anew to the persecuting storm; informers were goaded by increased rewards; and among thousands of less illustrious sufferers, Richard Baxter suffered joyfully the spoiling of his goods, and was condemned to what his ardent spirit did indeed feel bitterly, — a year of almost unbroken silence.[145] Owen, however, appears to have been left comparatively unmolested, — probably owing to the influences we have specified; and it is interesting to learn from an adversary with what zeal and constancy he employed his advantages to warn and succour the oppressed. "Witness his fishing out the king's counsels, and inquiring whether things went well to his great Diana, liberty of conscience? — how his majesty stood affected to it? — whether he would connive at it and the execution of the laws against it? — who were or could be made his friends at court? — what bills were like to be put up in Parliament? — how that assembly was united or divided? And according to the disposition of affairs he did acquaint his *under officers*; and they, by their letters each post, were to inform their fraternity in each corner of the kingdom how things were likely to go with them, how they should order their business, and either for a time omit or continue their conventicles."[146] Surely this was being able to find nothing against him, except as concerning the law of his God.

There was no sufferer in whose behalf Owen exerted his influence more earnestly than John Bunyan. It is well known that, as a preacher, Bunyan excited, wherever he went, an in-

---

145 Jenkyn's Essay on Life of Baxter, p. xx.

146 Letter to a Friend, p. 34. Orme, p. 274.

terest not surpassed even by the ministry of Baxter. When he preached in barns or on commons, he gathered eager thousands around him; and when he came to London, twelve hundred people would be found gathered together at seven on the dark morning of a winter working-day, to hear him expound the Word of God. Among these admiring multitudes Owen had often been discovered; — the most learned of the Puritans hung for hours, that seemed like moments, upon the lips of this untutored genius. The king is reported to have asked Owen, on one occasion, how a learned man like him could go "to hear a tinker prate;" to which the great theologian answered "May it please your majesty, could I possess the tinker's abilities for preaching, I would willingly relinquish all my learning."[147] For some years Bunyan's confinement in the prison of Bedford had, through the kindness of his good jailer, been attended with many mitigations; but towards the latter part of it, its severities had been greatly increased, and Owen used every effort to engage the interest of his old friend and tutor, Dr Barlow, for his release. Some of the details of this matter have been questioned by Southey, and its date is uncertain; but the leading facts seem above reasonable suspicion, and it is pleasing to know, that after some perplexing delay, Owen's interposition was successful in obtaining Bunyan's enlargement.[148]

During these chequered and anxious years, Owen's untiring pen had been as active as ever. In 1669 he had published "A brief Vindication of the Doctrine of the Trinity; as also, of the Person and Satisfaction of Christ;" a little treatise, containing the condensed substance of his great controversial work against Biddle and the Continental Socinians, — the *"Vindiciæ Evangelicæ."* There was wisdom in thus supplying the church with a less controversial manual on those vital questions. Many of Owen's larger works remind us of some ancient castle, with its embrasures and port-holes, admirably fitting it for the purposes

---

147 Hamilton's Life of Bunyan, p. xxix.

148 Asty, p. xxx. Southey's Life of Bunyan, p. lxiv.

of defence, but in the same degree rendering it unsuitable as a peaceful habitation. In little more than forty years after Owen's death, this little work had passed through seven editions.[149] In 1672 he had published "A Discourse concerning Evangelical Love, Church Peace and Unity," etc.; a work combining enlarged and generous sentiment with wise discrimination, and in which Owen enters at great length into the question respecting the occasional attendance of Nonconformists on the parish churches, — a question which found him and Baxter once more ranged on opposite sides.

And there were other works whose origin dated from this period, in which we can trace the faithful watchman, piously descrying the coming danger, or seeking to rear bulwarks against the already swelling tide. Two of these were precious fragments broken off from his great work on the Epistle to the Hebrews, and enlarged to meet present exigencies. The first was his "Treatise on the Sabbath;" in which he joined with Baxter, and all the other great writers among the Puritans, in seeking to preserve this precious fence, which the goodness of God has drawn around the vineyard of his church, and which he found assailed on the one hand by fanatics, who denounced it as a mere ceremonial and carnal observance, and by the more numerous and noisy disciples of the "Book of Sports," who hated it for its spirituality. The reader will be struck with the contrast between the Puritan Sabbath, as it is depicted in its staid and solemn cheerfulness by a Puritan divine, and as he often beholds it caricatured by the modern popular writer; and as he finds Owen arguing with the same classes of antagonists, and answering the same argument and objections as are rife at the present day, he will be disposed to subscribe to the theory, that errors have their orbits in which they move, and that their return may be calculated at a given juncture. The other work of this class to which we refer was, "The Nature and Punishment

---

149 Anon. Mem., p. xxix.

of Apostasy Declared, in an Exposition of Hebrews vi. 4–6."[150] It was emphatically a book for the times; when the multitudes who had merely played a part in religion in Cromwell's days had long since thrown off the mask, and taken amends for their restraints in the most shameless excesses; when to be sternly moral was almost to incur the suspicion of disloyalty; when to be called a Puritan was, with many, more discreditable than to be called a debauchee; and when the noon-day licentiousness of Charles' court, descending through the inferior ranks of life, carried every thing before it but what was rooted and grounded in a living piety.[151]

But the greatest work of Owen at this period was one which we leave its elaborate title to describe, — "A Discourse concerning the Holy Spirit; in which an account is given of his name, nature, personality, dispensation, operations, and effects. His whole work in the Old and New Creation is explained; the doctrine concerning it vindicated from opposition and reproaches. The nature and necessity also of Gospel holiness, the difference between grace and morality, or a spiritual life to God in evangelical obedience and a course of moral virtues, is stated and explained." The better part of two centuries have elapsed since this work of Owen's was given to the world, and yet no English work on the same vital subject has approached it in exhaustive fulness.[152] Wilberforce owns his obligations to it as one of his great theological textbooks; and Cecil declares that it had been

---

150 It is remarkable that in this treatise, p. 72–100, is to be found an explication of the last clause of the 6th verse of the 6th chapter of the Epistle to the Hebrews, which is strangely omitted in all editions of the "Exposition." The author has had this fact pointed out to him by his learned and venerated colleague, Dr Brown of Edinburgh.

151 Burnet's Own Times, i. 262–264.

152 An excellent posthumous work on the Holy Spirit, by the late Dr Jamieson of Edinburgh, edited with memoir by Rev. Andrew Sommerville, deserves to be better known. It displays more than one of the best qualities of Owen.

IV. His Retirement and Last Days

to him "a treasure-house" of divinity.[153] It was not merely the two common extremes of error that Owen grappled with in this masterly treatise, — that of the enthusiasts who talked of the inward light and of secret revelations, and that of the Socinians who did not believe that there was any Holy Ghost, and of whose scanty creed it has been severely said, that it is not likely often to become the faith of men of genius. There was a third class of writers at that time, from whom Owen apprehended more danger than either, — men who, in their preaching, dwelt much upon the credentials of the Bible, but little upon its truths, — who would have defended even the doctrine of the Holy Spirit as an article of their creed, and at the same time would have derided all reference to the actual work of divine grace upon a human heart as the "weak imagination of distempered minds." Much of Owen's treatise has reference to these accommodating and courtly divines, and is, in fact, a vindication of the reality of the spiritual life. He is not always able to repress his satire against these writers. Some of them had complained that they were reproached as "rational divines;" to which he replied, that if they were so reproached, it was, so far as he could discern, as Jerome was beaten by an angel for being a Ciceronian (in the judgment of some), very undeservedly.[154]

---

153 Cecil's Works, ii. 514 — Remains.

154 Address to the readers, p. xli. The whole of Owen's comprehensive plan, however, was not completed in this central treatise. New treatises continued to appear at intervals, giving to some important branch of this subject a more full discussion. In 1677 appeared "The Reason of Faith; or, an answer to the inquiry, Wherefore we believe the Scriptures to be the Word of God?" In 1678, "The Causes, Ways and Means of Understanding the mind of God as Revealed in his Word; and a declaration of the perspicuity of the Scriptures, with the external means of the interpretation of them." In 1682, "The Work of the Holy Spirit in Prayer; with a brief inquiry into the nature and use of mental prayers and forms." At length, in 1693, two posthumous discourses, "On the Work of the Sprit as a Comforter, and as he is the Author of Spiritual Gifts." filled up Owen's elaborate outlines. — Orme, p. 293.

Few glimpses are given us of Owen's domestic history; but it appears that, in January 1676, he was bereaved of his first wife. One of his early biographers says that she "was an excellent and comely person, very affectionate towards him, and met with suitable returns."[155] He remained a widower for about eighteen months, when he married a lady of the name of Michel, the daughter of a family of rank in Dorsetshire, and the widow of Thomas D'Oyley, Esq. of Chiselhampton, near Stadham. This lady brought Dr Owen a considerable fortune; which, with his own property, and a legacy that was left him about the same time by his cousin, Martyn Owen, made his condition easy, and even affluent, so that he was able to keep a carriage during his remaining years. On all which Anthony Wood remarks, with monkish spite, that "Owen took all occasions to enjoy the comfortable importances of this life."[156]

Many symptoms were now beginning to make it evident that Owen's public career was drawing to a close. The excitements and anxieties of a most eventful life, and the fatigues of severe study, were making themselves visible in more than one disease. Asthma afflicted him with such severity as often to unfit him for preaching; and stone, the frequent and agonizing disease of studious men in those times, gave no uncertain signs

---

155 Anon. Mem., p. xxxiv. Her epitaph by Mr Gilbert helps to fill up the portrait:—

"*Prima ætatis virilis consors Maria,*
Rei domesticæ perite studiosa.
Rebus Dei domus se totum addicendi;
Copiam illi fecit gratissimam."

There is a touching passage in a small work, remarkably well written, but little known, that leads us to think of Owen as an unusually tried parent. "His exercises by affliction were very great in respect of his children, none of whom he much enjoyed while living, and saw them all go off the stage before him." — Vindication of Owen by a friendly Scrutiny into the merits and manner of Mr Baxter's opposition to Twelve Arguments concerning Worship by the Liturgy, p. 38.

156 Wood's Athen. Oxon., iv. 100, 101.

of its presence. In these circumstances it became necessary to obtain assistants, both in the pastorate of the church in Leadenhall street, and also to act as his amanuenses in preparing his remaining works for the press among those who, for brief periods, were thus connected with him, we meet with the names of two persons of rather remarkable history, — Robert Ferguson, who, beginning his life as a minister, became at length a political intriguer and pamphleteer, and, after undertaking some perilous adventures in the cause of William, ultimately became a Jacobite, and ended his eccentric and agitated course with more of notoriety than of honour; and Alexander Shields, a Scotchman, whose antipathy to Prelacy was surpassed by his piety, and whose name Scottish Presbyterians still venerate as the author of the "Hind let Loose."[157] These two probably laboured with Owen principally in the capacity of amanuenses; but the amiable and excellent David Clarkson shared with him the duties of the pastorate, and rejoiced to divide the anxieties and toils, and soothe the declining years, of the illustrious Puritan. Clarkson evidently won the generous admiration of Baxter; and Dr Bates beautifully spoke of him as "a real saint, in whom the living spring of grace in his heart diffused itself in the veins of his conversation. His life was a silent repetition of his holy discourses."[158]

With the help of his amanuenses, Owen completed and published, in 1677, "The Doctrine of Justification by Faith, through the Imputation of the Righteousness of Christ, Explained, Confirmed, and Vindicated," — a work in which all the ratiocinative strength and command of resources of his best controversial days appear undiminished. We concur, indeed, to a certain extent, in the censure which has been charged against that part

---

[157] Orme, p. 301. Burnet sketches the character of Ferguson with his usual bold distinctness: "He was a hot and bold man, whose spirit was naturally turned to plotting," etc. — Own Times, i. 542.

[158] Funeral Sermon by Mr Bates on John xiv. 2, "In my Father's house are many mansions," &c. — Reliquæ Baxterianæ, part iii. p. 97.

of it which treats of the nature of justifying faith, as tending to perplex a subject whose very simplicity makes explanation equally impossible and unnecessary. The censure, however, ought not to be confined to Owen; for on the subject of faith the Puritan divines, with their scholastic distinctions, were far inferior to the theologians of the Reformation. The great difficulty about faith is not a metaphysical but a moral one; and there is truth in the observation, that elaborate attempts to describe it are like handling a beautiful transparency, whose lustre disappears whensoever it is touched.

This great work was probably the ripened fruit of many years of thought But as we examine the productions of Owen during the few remaining years of his life, it is easy to discover that they belonged principally to three classes, and two of those especially, owed their origin to events that were occurring around him, and to dangerous tendencies which his ever-vigilant eye was quick to discover. First, there were his various writings against Popery, such as his "Church of Rome no Safe Guide;" his "Brief and Impartial Account of the Protestant Religion;" and, in some degree also, his "Humble Testimony to the Goodness of God in his Dealing with Sinful Churches and Nations." In all of these we hear the watchman answering, "What of the night?" He is alive to the sympathies of Charles and his court with Popery, — to the readiness of not a few in the Church of England to move in the direction of Rome, — to the avowed so Romanism of the Duke of York, and his possible succession to the throne, — and to the dangers to religion, to liberty, and to every thing most dear to man, which these lowering evils portended. The wisdom and foresight of Dr Owen in many parts of these writings, which we now read in the light of subsequent events, strike us with surprise, often with admiration.

In addition to beholding the Protestants duly inspired and alarmed on the subject of Popery, Owen longed to see all alienations and divisions among them dispelled, and the various parts of the great Protestant community so united and mutually confiding, as to be prepared to resist their common

IV. His Retirement and Last Days

adversary. Not that he was the less convinced of the necessity and duty of separation from the Episcopal Church; for in a controversy with Stillingfleet, into which an ungenerous assault of that able Churchman drew him, he had produced one of his best defences of Nonconformity;[159] but he felt a growing desire, both to see the real differences between the various branches of the Nonconformist family reduced to their true magnitude, and, in spite of the differences that might, after all, remain, to behold them banded together in mutual confidence and united action. His work on "Union among Protestants" was written with this wise and generous design; and this, we are persuaded, was one of the chief ends contemplated by another work, — his "Inquiry into the Origin, Nature, Institution, Power, Order, and Communion of Evangelical Churches."[160] We are quite aware that some have represented this highly valuable treatise as a recantation of Dr Owen's views on church polity, and a return to those Presbyterian sentiments with which he had entered on his public life; but an examination of the treatise, we think, will make it evident that this was not in Owen's thoughts, and that his aim was rather to show how far he could come to meet the moderate Presbyterian, and to lay down a platform on which united action, in those times of trouble and of perils, which all division aggravated, could consistently take place. Accordingly we find him, while admirably describing the true nature of a

---

159 This was a bulky pamphlet, entitled, "A brief Vindication of Nonconformists from the Charge of Schism, as it was managed against them in a Sermon by Dr Stillingfleet." All the leading Nonconformists appear to have taken part in this controversy, from the grave Howe to witty Alsop. Stillingfleet replied in a clever work on the "Unreasonableness of Separation;" against which Owen brought his heavy artillery to bear with desolating effect, in "An Answer to the 'Unreasonableness of Separation,' and a Defence of the 'Vindication of the Nonconformists from the Guilt of Schism.'"

160 A second part of this treatise, "The True Nature of a Gospel Church, and its Government," was posthumous, and did not appear till 1689.

Gospel church, as a society of professed believers, and refusing to any man or body of men "all power of legislation in or over the church," avowing it as his conviction, that "the order of the officers which was so early in the primitive church, — viz. of one pastor or bishop in one church, assisted in rule and all holy ministrations with many elders, teaching or ruling only, — does not so overthrow church order as to render its rule or discipline useless." And in reference to the communion of churches, while repudiating every thing like authoritative interference and dictation on the part of any church or assembly of rulers, he holds that "no church is so independent that it can always, and in all cases, observe the duties it owes to the Lord Christ and the church catholic, by all those powers which it is able to act in itself distinctly, without conjunction of others; and the church which confines its duty to the acts of its own assemblies, cuts itself off from the external communion of the church catholic." He holds that "a synod convened in the name of Christ, by the voluntary consent of several churches concerned in mutual communion, may declare and determine of the mind of the Holy Ghost in Scripture, and decree the observation of things true and necessary, because revealed and appointed in the Scripture." And farther, that "if it be reported or known, by credible testimony, that any church has admitted into the exercise of divine worship any thing superstitious or vain, or if the members of it walk, like those described by the apostle, Phil. iii. 18, 19, unto the dishonour of the Gospel and of the ways of Christ, the church itself not endeavouring its own reformation and repentance, other churches walking in communion therewith, by virtue of their common interest in the glory of Christ and honour of the Gospel, after more private ways for its reduction, as opportunity and duty may suggest unto their elders, ought to assemble in a synod for advice, either as to the use of farther means for the recovery of such a church, or to withhold communion from it in case of obstinacy in its evil ways."[161] We

---

161 The True Nature of a Gospel Church, etc., chap. xi.

do not attempt to measure the distance between these principles and the Presbyterianism of Owen's day, or the diminished distance between them and the modified Presbyterianism of our own; but we state them, with one of Owen's oldest biographers, as an evidence of his "healing temper in this matter;"[162] and we even venture to suggest whether, at some future period of increased spirituality and external danger, they may not form the basis of a stable and honourable union among the two great evangelical sections of modern Nonconformists.

But besides the outward dangers to Protestantism, which made Owen so eager for union among his friends, we discover another and more interesting explanation still in the increased occupation of his mind with the great central truths of the Gospel, and his growing delight in them. The minor distinctions among Christians come to be seen by us in their modified proportions, when we have taken our place within the inner circle of those great truths which constitute the peculiar glory and power of Christianity; and this inner and more radiant circle formed more and more the home of Dr Owen's heart. This is evident from the three great doctrinal and devotional works which were produced by him at this period, and which we have yet to name.

First, there appeared his "Χριστολογία, or Declaration of the Glorious Mystery of the Person of Christ, God and man, with the infinite wisdom, love, and power of God in the constitution thereof. As also, of the grounds and reasons of his incarnation; the nature of his ministry in heaven; the present state of the church above thereon; and the use of his person in religion," etc. The root from which the whole discourse springs, is the memorable declaration of our Lord to Peter, Matt. xvi. 18, "And I say also unto thee, That thou art Peter, and upon this rock I will build my church; and the gates of hell shall not

---

[162] Anon. Mem., p. xxxiv. The same writer adds, in illustration of this healing temper, "I heard him say, before a person of quality and others, he could readily join with Presbytery as it was exercised in Scotland.

prevail against it:" — a declaration in which Owen finds three great truths, whose illustration forms the substance of the volume; — that the person of Christ is the foundation of his church; that opposition will be made by the powers of earth and hell to the church, as built on the person of Christ; and that the church built on the person of Christ shall never be separated from it or destroyed. It is easy to see what a rich field of doctrinal statement, learned illustration, and devout reflection, is opened for Owen's mind in these themes; and he expatiates in it with all the delight of a mind accustomed to high and heavenly communion. It is pleasing to mark how he casts off the cumbrous armour of a sometimes too scholastic style, that had kept him down in some of his earlier treatises; and, rising from the simply didactic into the devotional, aims to catch joyful glimpses of the glory that is soon to be revealed.

Then followed his heart-searching, heart-inspiring treatise on "The Grace and Duty of being Spiritually-minded," first preached to his own heart, and then to a private congregation; and which reveals to us the almost untouched and untrodden eminences on which Owen walked in the last years of his pilgrimage, — eminences for reaching which, it has been said by one of the humblest and holiest of men of our own times, "it would almost appear indispensable that the spiritual life should be nourished in solitude; and that, afar from the din, and the broil, and the tumult of ordinary life, the candidate for heaven should give himself up to the discipline of prayer and of constant watchfulness."[163]

The last production of Owen's pen was his "Meditations and Discourses on the Glory of Christ."[164] It embodies the holy musings of his latest days, and in many parts of it seems actually to echo the presses of the heavenly worshippers. We may ap-

---

163 Introductory Essay to Owen on Spiritual-mindedness, by Dr Chalmers, p. xxiv.

164 "Weakness, weariness, and the near approaches of death, do call me off from any farther labour in this kind." — Preface to reader.

IV. His Retirement and Last Days

ply to Owen's meditations, as recorded in this book, the words of Bunyan in reference to his pilgrim, — "Drawing near to the city, he had yet a more perfect view thereof." It is a striking circumstance, that each of the three great Puritan divines wrote a treatise on the subject of heaven, and that each had his own distinct aspect in which he delighted to view it. To the mind of Baxter, the most prominent idea of heaven was that of rest; and who can wonder, when it is remembered that his earthly life was little else than one prolonged disease? — to the mind of Howe, ever aspiring after a purer state of being, the favourite conception of heaven was that of holy happiness; — while to the mind of Owen, heaven's glory was regarded as consisting in the unveiled manifestation of Christ. The conceptions, though varied, are all true; and Christ, fully seen and perfectly enjoyed, will secure all the others. Let us now trace the few remaining steps that conducted Owen into the midst of this exceeding weight of glory.

We have already mentioned Lord Wharton, as one of those noblemen who continued their kindness to the Nonconformists in the midst of all their troubles. His country residence at Woburn, in Buckinghamshire, afforded a frequent asylum to the persecuted ministers; just as we find the castles of Mornay and De Plessis in France opened by their noble owners as a refuge to the Huguenots.

During his growing infirmities, Owen was invited to Woburn, to try the effect of change of air; and also that others of his persecuted brethren, meeting him in this safe retreat, might enjoy the benefit of united counsel and devotion. It appears that while here his infirmities increased upon him, and that he was unable to return to his flock in London at the time that he had hoped; and a letter written to them from this place, gives us so vivid a reflection of the anxieties of a period of persecution, and so interesting a specimen of Owen's fidelity and affection to his people, in the present experience of suffering, and in the dread of more, that we have peculiar delight in interweaving it with our narrative:—

"Beloved in the Lord, — Mercy, grace, and peace be multiplied to you from God our Father, and from our Lord Jesus Christ, by the communication of the Holy Ghost. I thought and hoped that by this time I might have been present with you, according to my desire and resolution; but it has pleased our holy gracious Father otherwise to dispose of me, at least for a season. The continuance of my painful infirmities, and the increase of my weaknesses, will not allow me at present to hope that I should be able to bear the journey. How great an exercise this is to me, considering the season, he knows, to whose will I would in all things cheerfully submit myself. But although I am absent from you in body, I am in mind, affection, and spirit, present with you, and in your assemblies; for I hope you will be found my crown and rejoicing in the day of the Lord; and my prayer for you night and day is, that you may stand fast in the whole will of God, and maintain the beginning of your confidence without wavering, firm unto the end. I know it is needless for me, at this distance, to write to you about what concerns you in point of duty at this season, that work being well supplied by my brother in the ministry; you will give me leave, out of my abundant affections towards you, to bring some few things to your remembrance, as my weakness will permit.

"In the first place, I pray God it may be rooted and fixed in our minds, that the shame and loss we may undergo for the sake of Christ and the profession of the Gospel is the greatest honour which in this life we can be made partakers of. So it was esteemed by the apostles, — they rejoiced that they were counted worthy to suffer shame for his name's sake. It is a privilege superadded to the grace of faith, which all are not made partakers of. Hence it is reckoned to the Philippians in a peculiar manner, that it was given to them, not only to believe in Christ, but also to suffer for him, — that it is far more hon-

IV. His Retirement and Last Days

ourable to suffer with Christ than to reign with the greatest of his enemies. If this be fixed by faith in our minds, it will tend greatly to our encouragement. I mention these things only, as knowing that they are more at large pressed on you.

"The next thing I would recommend to you at this season, is the increase of mutual love among yourselves; for every trial of our faith towards our Lord Jesus Christ is also a trial of our love towards the brethren. This is that which the Lord Christ expects from us, — namely, that when the hatred of the world does openly manifest and act itself against us all, we should evidence an active love among ourselves. If there have been any decays, any coldness herein, if they are not recovered and healed in such a season, it can never be expected. I pray God, therefore, that your mutual love may abound more and more in all the effects and fruits of it towards the whole society, and every member thereof. You may justly measure the fruit of your present trial by the increase of this grace among you; in particular, have a due regard to the weak and the tempted, — that that which is lame may not be turned out of the way, but rather let it be healed.

"Furthermore, brethren, I beseech you, hear a word of advice in case the persecution increases, — which it is like to do for a season. I could wish that, because you have no ruling elders, and your teachers cannot walk about publicly with safety, that you would appoint some among yourselves, who may continually, as their occasions will admit, go up and down, from house to house, and apply themselves peculiarly to the weak, the tempted, the fearful, — those that are ready to despond or to halt, and to encourage them in the Lord. Choose out those to this end who are endued with a spirit of courage and fortitude; and let them know that they are happy whom Christ will honour with this blessed work. And I desire the persons may be of this number who are faithful men, and know the state of the church; by this means you will know what is the frame of the members of the church, which will be a great direction to you, even in your prayers. Watch, now, brethren, that, if it be the will of God, not one soul may be lost from under your care. Let no one be overlooked or neglected; consider all their conditions, and apply yourselves to all their circumstances

"Finally, brethren, that I be not at present farther troublesome to you, examine yourselves as to your spiritual benefit which you have received, or do receive, by your present fears and dangers, which will alone give you the true measure of your condition; for if this tends to the exercise of your faith, and love, and holiness, if this increases your valuation of the privileges of the Gospel, it will be an undoubted token of the blessed issue which the Lord Christ will give unto your troubles. Pray for me, as you do; and do it the rather, that, if it be the will of God, I may be restored to you, — and if not, that a blessed entrance may be given to me into the kingdom of God and glory. Salute all the church in my name. I take the boldness in the Lord to subscribe myself your unworthy pastor, and your servant for Jesus' sake,

J. OWEN.

"P.S. — I humbly desire you would in your prayers remember the family where I am, from whom I have received, and do receive, great Christian kindness. I may say, as the apostle of Onesiphorus, 'The Lord give to them that they may find mercy of the Lord in that day, for they have often refreshed me in my great distress.'"

His infirmities increasing, he soon after removed from London to Kensington, for country air; occasionally, however, he was able still to visit London; and an incident which happened to him on one of these visits presents us with another picture of the times. As he was driving along the Strand, his carriage was stopped by two informers, and his horses seized. Greater violence would immediately have followed, had it not been that Sir Edmund Godfrey, a justice of the peace, was passing at the time, and seeing a mob collected round the carriage, asked what was the matter? On ascertaining the circumstances, he ordered the

IV. His Retirement and Last Days   117

informers, with Dr Owen, to meet him at the house of another
justice of the peace on an appointed day. When the day came, it
was found that the informers had acted so irregularly, that they
were not only disappointed of their base reward, but severely
reprimanded and dismissed. Thus once more did Owen escape
as a bird from the snare of the fowler.

Retiring still farther from the scenes of public life, Owen
soon after took up his abode in the quiet village of Ealing, where
he had a house of his own and some property. Only once again
did persecution hover over him, and threaten to disturb the sa-
credness of his declining days, by seeking to involve him and
some other of the Nonconformists in the Rye House plot; but
the charge was too bold to be believed, and God was about, ere
long, to remove him from the reach of all these evils, and to hide
him in his pavilion, from the pride of man and from the strife of
tongues. Anthony Wood has said of Owen that "he did very unwillingly lay down his head and die," but how different was the
spectacle of moral sublimity presented to the eyes of those who
were actual witnesses of the last days of the magnanimous and
heavenly-minded Puritan! In one of his latest writings, when referring to the near approach of the daily expected and earnestly desired hour of his discharge from all farther service in this
world, he had said, "In the continual prospect hereof do I yet
live, and rejoice; which, among other advantages unspeakable,
has already given me an inconcernment in those oppositions
which the passions or interests of men engage them in, of a very
near alliance unto, and scarce distinguishable from, that which
the grave will afford." And all the exercises of his deathbed
were the prolonged and brightening experience of what he here
describes. In a letter to his beloved friend Charles Fleetwood,
on the day before his death, he thus beautifully expresses his
Christian affection, and his good hope through grace:—

> "DEAR SIR, — Although I am not able to write one word my-
> self, yet I am very desirous to speak one word more to you
> in this world, and do it by the hand of my wife. The contin-

uance of your entire kindness, knowing what it is accompanied withal, is not only greatly valued by me, but will be a refreshment to me, as it is, even in my dying hour. I am going to Him whom my soul has loved, or rather who has loved me with an everlasting love, — which is the whole ground of all my consolation. The passage is very irksome and wearisome, through strong pains of various sorts, which are all issued in an intermitting fever. All things were provided to carry me to London today, according to the advice of my physicians; but we are all disappointed by my utter disability to undertake the journey. I am leaving the ship of the church in a storm; but whilst the great Pilot is in it, the loss of a poor under-rower will be inconsiderable. Live, and pray, and hope, and wait patiently, and do not despond; the promise stands invincible, that He will never leave us, nor forsake us. I am greatly afflicted at the distempers of your dear lady; the good Lord stand by her, and support and deliver her. My affectionate respects to her, and the rest of your relations, who are so dear to me in the Lord. Remember your dying friend with all fervency. I rest upon it that you do so, and am yours entirely,

J. OWEN."

The first sheet of his "Meditations on the Glory of Christ" had passed through the press under the superintendence of the Rev. William Payne, a Dissenting minister at Saffron Walden, in Essex; and on that person calling on him to inform him of the circumstance on the morning of the day he died, he exclaimed, with uplifted hands, and eyes looking upwards, "I am glad to hear it; but, O brother Payne! the long wished-for day is come at last, in which I shall see that glory in another manner than I have ever done, or was capable of doing, in this world."[165] Still it was no easy thing for that robust frame to be broken to pieces, and to let the struggling spirit go free. His physicians, Dr Cox and Sir Edmund King, remarked on the unusual strength of that earthly house which was about to be dissolved; while his

---

165 Middleton, iii. p. 480.

IV. His Retirement and Last Days

more constant attendants on that consecrated hour were awe-struck by the mastery which his mighty and heaven-supported spirit maintained over his physical agonies. "In respect of sicknesses, very long, languishing, and often sharp and violent, like the blows of inevitable death, yet was he both calm and submiss under all."[166] At length the struggle ceased; and with eyes and hands uplifted, as if his last act was devotion, the spirit of Owen passed in silence into the world of glory. It happened on the 24th of August 1683, the anniversary of St. Bartholomew's Day; — a day memorable in the annals of the Church of Christ, as that in which the two thousand Nonconformist confessors had exposed themselves to poverty and persecution at the call of conscience, and in which heaven's gates had been opened wide to receive the martyred Protestants of France. Eleven days afterwards, a long and mournful procession, composed of more than sixty noblemen, in carriages drawn by six horses each, and of many others in mourning coaches and on horseback, silently followed the mortal remains of Owen along the streets of London, and deposited them in Bunhill-fields, — the Puritan necropolis.[167]

"We have had a light in this candlestick," said the amiable David Clarkson, on the Sabbath following; "we have had a light in this candlestick, which did not only enlighten the room, but gave light to others far and near: but it is put out. We did not sufficiently value it. I wish I might not say that our sins have put it out. We had a special honour and ornament, such as other churches would much prize; but the crown has fallen from our heads, — yea, may I not add, 'Woe unto us, for we have sinned?'"[168]

Dr Owen had only reached the confines of old age when he died; but the wonder is, that a life of such continuous ac-

---

166 Vindication of Owen by a friendly Scrutiny, etc., p. 38.

167 Stoughton's Spiritual Heroes.

168 "Funeral Sermon on the most lamented death of the late reverend and learned John Owen, D.D., preached the next Lord's day after his interment." By David Clarkson, B.D.

tion and severe study had not sooner burned out the lamp. It may be remarked of him, as Andrew Fuller used to say of himself, that "he possessed a large portion of being." He is said to have stooped considerably during the later years of his life; but when in his full vigour, his person was tall and majestic, while there was a singular mixture of gravity and sweetness in the expression of his countenance. His manners were courteous; his familiar conversation, though never deficient in gravity, was pleasantly seasoned with wit; and he was admired by his friends for his remarkable command of temper under the most annoying provocations, and his tranquil magnanimity in the midst of all the changes of fortune to which, in common with all his great Puritan contemporaries, he was exposed. "His general frame was serious, cheerful, and discoursive, — his expressions savouring nothing of discontent, much of heaven and love to Christ, and saints, and all men; which came from him so seriously and spontaneously, as if grace and nature were in him reconciled, and but one thing."[169] Such is the portrait of Owen that has descended to us from those who best "knew his manner of life;" and our regret is all the greater, that we are constrained to receive the description in this general form, and that biography has opened to us so few of those glimpses of his domestic and social life which would have enabled us to "catch the living manners as they rose," and to fill up for ourselves the less strongly defined outlines of his character.

Our business, however, is more with Dr Owen in his various public relations, and it seems to be a fit conclusion of this Memoir, that we should now attempt, in a few closing paragraphs, to express the estimate which a review of his conduct in these relations warrants us to form of his character. One of the most natural errors into which a biographer is in danger of being betrayed, is that of asserting the superiority of the individual who has been the subject of his memoir to all his contemporaries; and it would probably require no great stretch of ingenuity or

---

169 Vindication of Owen by a friendly Scrutiny, etc., p. 38.

IV. His Retirement and Last Days

eloquent advocacy to bring out Dr Owen as at least "primus inter pares." In finding our way, however, to such conclusions, almost every thing depends on the particular excellence on which we fix as our standard of judgment; and we are persuaded that were we allowed to select a separate excellence in each case our standard, we could bring out each of the three great Puritans as, in his turn, the greatest. Let impressive eloquence in the pulpit and ubiquitous activity out of it be the standard, and all this crowned with successes truly apostolical, and must not every preacher of his age yield the palm to Richard Baxter? Or let our task be to search for the man in that age of intellectual giants who was most at home in the *philosophy* of Christianity, whose imagination could bear every subject he touched upwards into the sunlight, and cover it with the splendours of the firmament, and would we not lay the crown at the feet of the greatly good John Howe? But let the question be, who among all the Puritans was the most remarkable for his intimate and profound acquaintance with the truths of revelations who could shed the greatest amount of light upon a selected portion of the Word of God, discovering its hidden riches, unfolding its connections and harmonies, and bringing the most abstruse doctrines of revelation to bear upon the conduct and the life who was the "interpreter, one amongst a thousand?" or let other excellencies that we are about to specify be chosen as the standard, and will not the name of Dr Owen, in this case, obtain an unhesitating and unanimous suffrage? Such a mode, therefore, of expressing our estimate is not only invidious, but almost certain to fail, after all, in conveying a distinct and accurate conception of the character we commend. We prefer, therefore, to contemplate Dr Owen in his principal relations and most prominent mental features, and to paint a portrait without fashioning an idol.

The first excellence we have to name is one in regard to which, we are persuaded, the modern popular estimate has fallen considerably below the truth. We refer to the qualities of Owen as a preacher. No one who is familiar with his printed sermons, and has marked the rich ore of theology with which they abound, will refuse to him the praise of a great sermon-maker; but this gift is not always found united in the same person with that other excellence which is equally necessary to constitute the preacher, — the power, namely, of expressing all the sentiment and feeling contained in the words by means of the living voice. And the general impression seems to be, that Dr Owen was deficient in this quality, and that his involved sentences, though easily overlooked in a composition read in secret, must, without the accompaniments of a most perfect delivery, have been fatal to their effect upon a public audience. It is even supposed that his intellectual habits must have been unfavourable to his readiness as an orator, and that while, like Addison, he had abundance of gold in the bank, he was frequently at a loss for ready money. But Owen's contemporaries report far differently; and the admiring judgment of some of them is the more to be relied on, that, as in the case of Anthony Wood, it was given with a grudge. Their descriptions, indeed, would lead us to conclude his eloquence was of the persuasive and insinuating, rather than, like Baxter's, of the impassioned kind, — the dew, and not the tempest; but in this form of eloquence he appears to have reached great success. His amiable colleague, Mr Clarkson, speaking of "the admirable facility with which he could discourse on any subject," describes him as "never at a loss for language, and better expressing himself extempore than others with premeditation;" and retaining this felicity of diction and mastery of his thoughts "in the presence even of the highest persons in the nation." We have already had occasion to quote Wood's representation of Owen's oratory, as "moving and winding the affections of his auditory almost as he pleased;"[170] and a writer of great judgment and discrimination, who had often heard Owen preach, speaks of him as "so great an ornament to the pulpit, that, for matter, manner, and

---

[170] The words seems to be Dodwell's, but they are quoted by Wood with approval.

IV. His Retirement and Last Days

efficacy on the hearers, he represented indeed an ambassador of the Most High, a teacher of the oracles of God. His person and deportment were so genteel and graceful, that rendered him when present as affecting, or more than his works and fame when absent. This advanced the lustre of his internal excellencies, by shining through so bright a lantern."

Indeed, the sermons of Owen and his compeers, not only compel us to form a high estimate of the preachers, but of the hearers of those times, who could relish such strong meat, and invite its repetition. And seldom perhaps on earth has a preacher been called to address more select audiences than Owen. We do not now refer to the crowding multitudes that hailed his early ministry at Fordham and Coggeshall, or to those little secret audiences meeting in upper chambers, to whom truth was whispered rather than proclaimed, but to those high intellects that were wont to assemble around him at Oxford, and to those helmed warriors and heroes of the commonwealth, who, on days of public fasting and thanksgiving, or on high occasions of state, would stand in groups to hear the great Puritan discourse. Many of these earnest souls were no sciolists in divinity themselves, and had first drawn their swords to secure the liberty of prophesying and uncontrolled freedom of worship.

We should form a very imperfect estimate of the character of Dr Owen, and of the beneficent influence which he exerted, did we not advert to his greatness as a man of affairs. In this respect we need have no hesitation in asserting his superiority to all the Puritans. Attached from principle to that great party whose noble mission it was to assert and to vindicate the rights of conscience and freedom of worship, he soon rose to be its chief adviser on all occasions of great practical exigency. He combined in a remarkable degree that clear perception and firm grasp of great abstract principles, that quick discernment of character and detection of hidden motive in others, which acts in some men with all the promptitude and infallibility of instinct, — that fertility of resources, that knowledge of the times for vigorous action and of the times in which to economize strength, which, when found in great prominence and happy combination in the politician, fit him for the high duties of statesmanship. He was the man who, by common consent, was called to the helm in a storm. Baxter was deficient in more than one of those qualities which are necessary to such a post; while his ardent nature would, on some occasions, have betrayed him into practical excesses, and at other times his love of nice and subtle distinction would have kept him discussing when he should have been acting; — while Howe's elevation above the affairs of daily life, his love of solitude, which made him almost wish even to die alone in some unfrequented wood, or on the top of some far remote mountain, disinclined, if it did not unfit him, for the conduct of public affairs. But Owen's singular excellence in this respect was early manifested, — and to no eye sooner than to that of Cromwell. We have seen him inviting his counsels on the affairs of Dublin University; taking him with him to Scotland, not only as his chaplain, but as his adviser in the affairs of that campaign, when he found it more difficult to manage its theologians than to conquer its armies; and at length intrusting to him the arduous and almost desperate enterprise of presiding over Oxford, and raising it from its ruins. And throughout more than thirty years of the long struggle of the Puritans and Nonconformists, he was the counsellor and presiding mind, to whom all looked in the hour of important action and overwhelming difficulty.

Some have accused Owen and other Nonconformists of his age as too political for their office. But who made them such? Was it not the men who were seeking to wrest from them their dearest civil rights, and to make it a crime to worship God according to their consciences? With such base ingenuity of reproach were the Huguenots of France accused of holding secret meetings, after they had been forbidden to meet in public. It was no small part of Owen's praise, that he saw and obeyed the necessity of his position; and that perhaps, of all the Puritans of his age, he was the most quick to "observe the signs of the times, and to know what Israel ought to do." This is the

IV. His Retirement and Last Days

estimate we should be disposed to form from a simple retrospect of the facts of our narrative; but it appears to have been the judgment which some of the best of Owen's contemporaries were not slow to express. In that admirable letter to Baxter from which we have already quoted, referring more particularly to Owen's vice-chancellorship, the writer says, "And though his years, piety, principles, and strait discipline, with the interest he adhered to, affected many of the heads and students with contempt, envy, and enmity at the first; his personal worth, obliging deportment, and dexterity in affairs that concerned him in that station, so mastered all, that the university grew not only content with, but proud of such a vice-chancellor. And, indeed, such were his temper and accomplishments, that whatever station or sort of men his lot, choice, or interest, should place him in or among, it were no small wonder that he were not uppermost:— that was his proper sphere, which those with whom he was concerned generally courted him into, and few envied or corrived."[171]

But the aspect in which we most frequently think of Owen, and from which our highest estimate of him is formed, is that of a theological writer. Even the mere material bulk of his works fills us with surprise; and when we consider the intensely active life which Owen led, their production strikes us as almost incredible. In Russell's editions together with the edition of his "Exposition" by Wright, his works fill no fewer than twenty-eight goodly octavo volumes, though we almost sympathize with the feeling that the folio form, in which many of them originally appeared, more fitly represents their intellectual stature. "Hew down the pyramids," says Sir James Stephen, with a feeling which every lover of the old divinity will understand, — "Hew down the pyramids into a range of streets! divide Niagara into a succession of water privileges! — but let not the spirits of the mighty dead be thus evoked from their majestic

---

171 "Corrived" is an obsolete English word for "rivalled."

shrines to animate the dwarfish structures of our bookselling generation."

It is only, however, when we have acquired some considerable familiarity with the contents of these volumes, and when we remember that on almost every one of the great controversies, — such as the Arminian, the Socinian, the Popish, and the Episcopalian, — he has produced works which, after the lapse of nearly two centuries, are still regarded by unanimous consent as masterpieces on the themes on which they treat, that we feel unhesitating confidence in placing the name of Owen among the first names of that age of amazing intellectual achievement. In some of his controversies he had to do with men of inferior ability, of whom it might be said, as of some of Fuller's opponents, that "they scarcely served him for a breakfast;" but in other controversies, such as that with Goodwin on the perseverance of the saints, he was called to grapple with some of the best and most accomplished men of his age. But he never quailed before any opponent. More than one of his works put an end to the controversy by driving his adversaries to despair; and only once — viz., in his rash encounter with Walton — did he retire undeniably vanquished from the field. It is unnecessary to repeat observations that have been made in the narrative on Owen's various works; but this seems to be the place at which to indicate what seem to have been the most distinguishing qualities of Owen as a theological writer.

Perhaps no better word could be found to express one of the most striking characteristics of Owen, than that which Mackintosh has used to describe the writings of Bentham, — *exhaustiveness*. He goes through his subject "in the length thereof, and in the breadth thereof." It was his custom to read all the works that had been written on his particular subject, — especially the writings of opponents, — and then to pass deliberately from point to point of his theme, and bring the whole concentrated light of Scripture to bear upon its elucidation and establishment. He leaves nothing to be added by one who shall follow in the same path, not even little gleanings at the corners of the field.

— We venture to describe another feature of Owen's works by the phrase, Theological conservatism. In an age remarkable for its intellectual excitement, which gave birth to all manner of extravagances in opinion, like the ocean in a storm, bringing to the surface monsters, and hydras, and chimeras dire, and then producing in due season a reaction into the shallows of Rationalism, Owen displayed no disposition to change. There is no writer in whose opinions throughout life there is more of consistency and unity. There is everywhere visible strong intellect and profound thought; but it is intellect, not sporting itself with novelties, and expending itself in presumptuous speculation, but reasoning out and defending what apostles taught, and feeling that there is enough in this to fill an angel's grasp. Various causes combined to work out this quality in Owen, especially his profound reverence for the authority of Scripture, leading him to travel over its ample field, but restraining him from passing beyond it; the influence of the truth upon his own heart, as a living power writing its divine witness within him; and also his vast learning, which enabled him to trace opinions to their source, and to detect in that which the ignorant and half-learned looked upon as a dazzling discovery, the resurrection of an exploded error, whose only novelty was in its name.

Allied to this, and in part accounting for it, was what we would style the devout Calvinism of Owen's cast of thought. Baxter and he held substantially the same truths, their views, even when they seemed the most divergent, differing in form and complexion more than in substance; but still it is evident that the two great men had each his distinct and favourite standing-point. With Baxter, the initial thought was man in need of a great restorative system; and this led him outwards and upwards, from step to step of the Christian salvation. The initial thought with Owen was God in the past eternity devising a scheme of salvation through a Mediator; which he unfolded in its wondrous arrangements and provisions from age to age of the world, and whose glorious results were to continue to be enjoyed for ever and ever. This gave a comprehensiveness and an elevation to Owen's whole theology, and accounts in part for the fact that Baxter seems greatest when bearing upon the duties of the sinner, and calling him to repentance, — "now or never;" while Owen comes forth in his greatest strength when instructing and building up those who have already believed.

And this suggests another of his most remarkable excellencies, — the power, namely, of bringing the various doctrines of the Christian system, even the most abstruse, to bear, in the form of motive and consolation, upon the affections and active powers of our human nature. Great as Owen is when we see him as the gigantic polemic, putting forth his intellectual might in "earnestly contending for the faith once delivered unto the saints;" we have not seen him in all his greatness until, in such practical works as his treatise on the "Mortification of Sin in Believers," he brings the truth into contact, not so much with the errors of the heretic, as with the corruption and deceitfulness of the human heart. Then we have hesitated which most to admire, — his intimate knowledge of the Word of God, or his profound acquaintance with the heart of man, or the skill with which he brings the one into vigorous and healing action upon the other; while all his great qualities, as the expositor of the Scriptures, as the defender of the faith, as the profound theologian, and as the wise practical instructor, have seemed to manifest themselves at once in single and united greatness, in that noble intellectual pyramid, his "Exposition of the Epistle to the Hebrews."

Yet some of the excellencies that we have named stand closely connected with Owen's chief defect, — which is to be found in his manner, rather than in his matter. His wish to exhaust his particular theme has made him say every thing on a subject that could be said, and betrayed him into an occasional prolixity and discursiveness, the absence of which would have made his works far more popular, and far more useful. He wants *perspective* in composition, and does not seem to know the secret of touching on themes, without laboriously handling them. This, with an occasionally involved and parenthetical style, has

IV. His Retirement and Last Days

formed, as we conceive, the chief barrier to Owen's yet wider acceptance. The sentiment of Dr Vaughan is a just one, that had the fluency and elegance of Bates been united to the massive thoughts of Owen, we should have had a near approach to the perfect theological writer. But let us admit this occasional defect; and let us even farther concede, that in other qualities he is not equal to others of the Puritans, — that he is surpassed by Baxter in point and energy, by Flavel in tenderness, by Howe in majesty, by both the Henrys in proverb and epigram, by Bates in beautiful similitudes; — still, where shall we find, in the theological writers of his own or of any age, so much of the accumulated treasures of a sanctified learning, — of the mind of God clearly elucidated and invincibly defended, — of profound and massive thought? His works are like a soil which is literally impregnated with gold, and in which burnished masses of the virgin ore are sure to reward him who patiently labours in it.

John Owen belonged to a class of men who have risen from age to age in the church, to represent great principles, and to revive in the church the life of God. The supreme authority of the Scriptures in all matters of religion, — the headship of Christ, — the rights of conscience, — religion as a thing of spirit, and not of form, resulting from the personal belief of certain revealed truths, and infallibly manifesting itself in a holy life, — the church as a society distinct from the world; — these principles, often contended for in flames and blood, were the essence of that Puritanism which found one of its noblest examples in Owen. Puritanism, it has been finely said, was the feeling of which Protestantism was the argument. But even then, it was an old spirit under a new name, which, heaven-enkindled, has ever borne the two marks of its celestial origin, in blessing the world and being persecuted by it. It was the spirit which breathed in the Lollards of Germany; in the Hussites of Bohemia, — in those saints, who

"On the Alpine mountains cold,
  Kept God's truth so pure of old,
  When all our fathers worshipp'd stocks and stones;"

in the Huguenots of France; and in the stern Scottish Covenanters; — and which God has sometimes sent down since, like a benignant angel, when the church at any time has begun to stagnate in a cold orthodoxy, to trouble the waters of the sanctuary, that the lame might be healed. It is a spirit which the inert orthodoxy and the superficial evangelism of the church even now greatly needs to have breathed into it from heaven. And the laborious and prayerful study of the writings of the Puritans might do much to restore it. Only let the same truths be believed with the same faith, and they will produce the same men, and accomplish the same intellectual and moral miracles. A due appreciation of the most pressing wants of our age, and a timely discernment of its most serious perils, would draw from us the prayer which is said to have once escaped the lips even of the cold and calculating Erasmus, — "*O, sit anima mea cum Puritanis Anglicanis!*"

Appendix to the Life of Dr Owen

I. Epitaph Inscribed on the Monument of Dr Owen in Bunhill-fields

JOHANNES OWEN, S. T. P.
Agro Oxoniensi Oriundus;
Patre insigni Theologo Theologus Ipse Insignior;
Et Seculi hujus Insignissimis annumerandus:
Communibus Humaniorum Literarum Suppetiis,
Mensura parum Communi, Instructus;
Omnibus, quasi bene Ordinata Ancillarum Serie,
Ab illo jussis Suæ Famulari Theolgiæ:
Theologiæ Polemicæ, Practicæ, &, quam vocant, Casuum
(Harum enim Omnium, quæ magis Sua habenda erat, ambigitur)
In illa, Viribus plusquam Herculeis, Serpentibus tribus,
Arminio, Socino, Cano, Venenosa Strinxit Guttera:
In ista, Suo prior, ad Verbi Amussim, Expertus Pectore,
Universam, Sp. S$^{cti.}$ Œconomiam Aliis tradidit:
Et missis Cæteris, Coluit Ipse, Sensitque,
Beatam, quam Scripsit, cum Deo Communionem:
In Terris Viator comprehensori in Cœlis proximus:
In Casuum Theologia, Singulis Oraculi instar habitus;
Quibus Opus erat, & Copia, Consulendi:
Scriba ad Regnum Cœlorum usquequoque Institutus;
Multis privatos infra Parietes, à Suggesto Pluribus,
A Prelo Omnibus, ad eundem Scopum collineantibus,
Pura Doctrinæ Evangelicæ Lampas Præluxit;
Et sensim, no sine aliorum, suoque sensu,

Sic prælucendo Periit,
Assiduis Infirmitatibus Obsiti,
Morbis Creberrimis Impetiti,
Durisque Laboribus potissimum Attriti, Corporis
(Fabricæ, donec ita Quassatæ, Spectabilis) Ruinas,
Deo ultrà Serviendo inhabiles, Sancta Anima,
Deo ultrà Fruendi Cupida, Deseruit;
Die, à Terrenis Potestatibus, Plurimis facto Fatali;
Illi, à Cœlesti Numine, Felici reddito;

Mensis Scilicet Augusti XXIV^Q. Anno à Partu Virgineo.
MDCLXXXIII^Q, Ætat. LXVII^Q.

Translation

John Owen, D.D., born in the county of Oxford, the son of an eminent minister, himself more eminent, and worthy to be enrolled among the first divines of the age; furnished with human literature in all its kinds, and in its highest degrees, he called forth all his knowledge in an orderly train to serve the interests of religion, and minister in the sanctuary of his God. In divinity, practic, polemic, and casuistical, he excelled others, and was in all equal to himself. The *Arminian, Socinian,* and *Popish* errors, those *hydras,* whose contaminated breath and deadly poison infested the church, he, with more than *Herculean* labour, repulsed, vanquished, and destroyed. The whole economy of redeeming grace, revealed and applied by the Holy Spirit, he deeply investigated, and communicated to others, having first felt its divine energy, according to its draught in the holy Scriptures, transfused into his own bosom. Superior to all terrene pursuits, he constantly cherished, and largely experienced, that blissful communion with Deity he so admirably describes in his writings. While on the road to heaven, his elevated mind almost comprehended its full glories and joys. When he was consulted on cases of conscience, his resolutions contained the wisdom of an oracle. He was a scribe every way instructed in the mysteries of the kingdom of God. In conversation he held up to *many*, in his public discourses to *more*, in his publications from the press to *all*, who were set out for the celestial *Zion*, the effulgent lamp of evangelical truth, to guide their steps to immortal glory. While he was thus diffusing his divine light, with his own inward sensations, and the observations of his afflicted friends, his earthly tabernacle gradually decayed, till at length his deeply-sanctified soul, longing for the fruition of its God, quitted the body. In younger age, a most comely and majestic form; but in the latter stages of life, depressed by constant infirmities, emaciated with frequent diseases, and above all crushed under the weight of intense and unremitting studies, it became an incommodious mansion for the vigorous exertions of the spirit in the service of its God. He left the world on a day dreadful to the church by the cruelties of men, but blissful to himself by the plaudits of his God, August 24, 1683, aged 67. — *Translated by Dr Gibbons.*

II. Some Letters

The following LETTERS embrace all the Correspondence of DR OWEN which has been preserved, and is of any importance:—

To M. Du Moulin

SIR, — I have received your strictures upon our Confession, wherein you charge it with palpable contradiction, nonsense, enthusiasm, and false doctrine, — that is, all the evils that can be crowded into such a writing; and I understand, by another letter since, that you have sent the same paper to others, — which is the sole cause of the return which I now make to you; and I beg your pardon in telling you, that all your instances are your own mistakes, or the mistakes of your friend, as I shall briefly manifest to you.

First, you say there is a plain contradiction between chap. iii. art. 6, and chap. xxx. art. 2. In the first place it is said, "None but the elect are redeemed;" but in the other it is said, "The sacrament is a memorial of the one offering of Christ upon the cross for all." I do admire to find this charged by you as a contradiction; for you know full well that all our divines who maintain that the elect only were redeemed effectually by Christ, do yet grant that Christ died for all, in the Scripture sense of the word, — that is, some of all sorts, — and never dreamt of any contradiction in their assertion. But your mistake is worse; for in chap. xxx. art. 2, which you refer to, there is not one word mentioned of Christ's dying for all; but that the sacrifice which he offered was offered once for all, — which is the expression of the apostle, to intimate that it was but once offered, in opposition to the frequent repetitions of the sacrifices of the Jews. And pray, if you go on in your translation, do not fall into a mistake upon it; for in the very close of the article it is said, "That Christ's only sacrifice was a propitiation for the sins of all the elect." The words you urge out of 2 Pet. ii. 1, are not in the text: they are, by your quotation, "Denied him that had redeemed them;" but it is, "Denied the sovereign Lord which had bought them;" — which words have quite another sense.

Something you quote out of chap. vi. art. 6, where I think you suppose we do not distinguish between the *"reatus"* and *"macula"* of sin; and do think that we grant the defilement of Adam's person, and consequently of all intermediate propagations, to be imputed unto us. Pray, sir, give me leave to say, that I cannot but think your mind was employed about other things when you dreamt of our being guilty of such a folly and madness; neither is there any one word in the Confession which gives countenance unto it. If you would throw away so much time as to read any part of my late discourse about justification, it is not unlikely but that you would see something of the nature of the guilt of sin, and the imputation of it, which may give you satisfaction.

In your next instance, which you refer unto chap. xix. art. 3, by some mistake (there being nothing to the purpose in that place), you say, "It is presupposed that some who have attained age may be elected, and yet have not the knowledge of Jesus Christ; which is a pure enthusiasm, and is contrary to chap. xx. art. 2." Why, sir! that many who are eternally elected, and yet for some season — some less, some longer — do live without the knowledge of Christ, until they are converted by the Word and Spirit, is not an enthusiasm; but your exception is contrary to the whole Scripture, contrary to the experience of all days and ages, overthrows the work of the ministry, and is so absurd to sense, and reason, and daily experience, that I know not what to say to it; only, I confess that if, with some of the Arminians, you do not believe that any are elected from eternity, or before they do actually believe, something may be spoken to countenance your exception: but that we cannot regard, for it was our design to oppose all their errors.

Your next instance is a plain charge of false doctrine, taken out of chap. xi. art. 1, speaking, as you say, of the active obedience of Christ imputed to us, which is contrary to art. 3, where it is said that Christ acquits by his obedience in death, and not by his fulfilling of the law. Sir, you still give me cause of some new admiration in all these objections, and I fear you make use of some corrupt copy of our Confession; — for we say not, as you allege, that Christ by his obedience in death did acquit us, and not by his fulfilling of the law; but we say that Christ, by his obedience and death, did fully discharge the debt of all those who are justified, — which comprehends both his active and passive righteousness. But you add a reason, whereby you design to disprove this doctrine of our concerning the imputation of the active righteousness of Christ unto our justification. Why, you say, it is contrary to reason; for that we are freed from satisfying God's justice by being punished by death, but not from the fulfilling of the law: therefore the fulfilling of the law by Christ is no satisfaction for us, — we are not freed from active obedience, but from passive obedience. Pray, sir, do not mistake that such mistaken reasonings can give us any occasion to change our judgments in an article of truth of this importance. When you shall have been pleased to read my book of Justification, and have answered solidly what I have written upon this subject, I will tell you more of my mind. In the meantime I tell you, we are by the death of Christ freed from all sufferings as they are purely penal, and the effect of the curse, though they spring out of that root; only, sir, you and I know full well that we are not freed from pains, afflictions, and death itself, — which had never been, had they not proceeded from the curse of the law. And so, sir, by the obedience of Christ we are freed from obedience to the law, as to justification by the works thereof. We are no more obliged to obey the law in order to justification than we are obliged to undergo the penalties of the law to answer its curse. But these things have been fully debated elsewhere.

In the last place, your friend wishes it could be avoided, and declined to speak any thing about universal grace, for that it would raise some or most divines against it. I judge myself beholden to your friend for the advice, which I presume he judges to be good and wholesome; but I beg your pardon that I cannot comply with it, although I shall not reflect with any severity upon them who are of another judgment; and, to tell you the truth, the immethodical new method introduced to give countenance to universal grace, is, in my judgment, suited to draw us off from all due conceptions concerning the grace of God in Jesus Christ; which I shall not now stay to demonstrate, though I will not decline the undertaking of it, if God gives me strength, at any time. And I do wonder to hear you say that many, if not most divines, will rise against it, who have published in print that there were but two in England that were of that opinion, and have strenuously opposed it yourself. How things are in France, I know not; but at Geneva, in Holland, in Switzerland, in all the Protestant churches of Germany, I do know that this universal grace is exploded. Sir, I shall trouble you no farther. I pray be pleased to accept of my desire to undeceive you in those things, wherein either a corrupt copy of our Confession or the reasonings of other men have given you so many mistaken conceptions about our Confession. — I am, Sir, yours,

J. OWEN.

To the Lady Hartopp

DEAR MADAM, — Every work of God is good; the Holy One in the midst of us will do no iniquity; and all things shall work together for good unto them that love him, even those things which at present are not joyous, but grievous; only his time is to be waited for, and his way submitted unto, that we seem not to be displeased in our hearts that he is Lord over us. Your dear infant is in the eternal enjoyment of the fruits of all our prayers; for the covenant of God is ordered in all things, and sure. We shall go to her; she shall not return to us. Happy she was in this above us, that she had so speedy an issue of sin and misery, being born only to exercise your faith and patience, and to glorify God's grace in her eternal blessedness. My trouble would be great on the account of my absence at this time from you both, but that this also is the Lord's doing; and I know my own uselessness wherever I am. But this I will beg of God for you both that you may not faint in this day of trial, — that you may have a clear view of those spiritual and temporal mercies wherewith you are yet intrusted (all undeserved), — that sorrow of the world may not so overtake your hearts as to disenable to any duties, to grieve the Spirit, to prejudice your lives; for it tends to death. God in Christ will be better to you than ten children, and will so preserve your remnant, and to add to them, as shall be for his glory and your comfort.

Only consider that sorrow in this case is no duty, it is an effect of sin, whose cure by grace we should endeavour. Shall I say, Be cheerful? I know I may. God help you to honour grace and mercy in a compliance therewith. My heart is with you, my prayers shall be for you, and I am, dear madam, your most affectionate friend and unworthy pastor,

J. OWEN.

To Mrs Polhill

DEAR MADAM, — The trouble expressed in yours is a great addition to mine; the sovereignty of divine wisdom and grace is all that I have at this day to retreat unto; God direct you thereunto also, and you will find rest and peace. It adds to my trouble that I cannot possibly come down to you this week. Nothing but engaged duty could keep me from you one hour: yet I am conscious how little I can contribute to your guidance in this storm, or your satisfaction. Christ is your pilot; and however the vessel if tossed whilst he seems to sleep, he will arise and rebuke these winds and waves in his own time. I have done it, and yet shall farther wrestle with God for you, according to the strength he is pleased to communicate. Little it is which at this distance I can mind you of; yet some few things are necessary. Sorrow not too much for the dead: she is entered into rest, and is taken away from the evil to come. Take heed lest, by too much grief, you too much grieve that Holy Spirit, who is infinitely more to us than all natural relations. I blame you not that you so far attend to the call of God in this dispensation as to search yourself, to judge and condemn yourself: grace can make it an evidence to you that you shall not be judged or condemned of the Lord. I dare not say that this chastisement was not needful. We are not in heaviness unless need be; but if God be pleased to give you a discovery of the wisdom and care that is in it, and how needful it was to awaken and restore your soul in any thing, perhaps in many things, in due time you will see grace and love in it also. I verily believe God expects, in this dealing with you, that you should judge yourself, your sins and your decays; but he would not have you misjudge your condition. But we are like froward children, who, when they are rebuked and corrected, neglect other things, and only cry that their parents hate and reject them. You are apt to fear, to think and say, that you are one whom God regards not, who are none of his; and that for sundry reasons which you suppose you can plead. But, saith God, this is not the business; this is a part of your frowardness. I call you to quicken your grace, to amend your own ways; and you think you have nothing to do but to question my love. Pray, madam, my dear sister, child and care, beware you lose not the advantage of this dispensation; you will do so, if you use it only to afflictive sorrows, or questioning of the love of God, or your interest in Christ.

The time will be spent in these things which should be taken up in earnest endeavours after a compliance with God's will, quickenings of grace, returns after backsliding, mortification of sin and love of the world, until the sense of it do pass away. Labour vigorously to bring your soul to this twofold resolution:— 1. That the will of God is the best rule for all things, and their circumstances. 2. That you will bring yourself into a fresh engagement to live more to him: and you will find the reminder of your work easy; for it is part of the yoke of Christ. I shall trouble you no farther but only to give you the assurance that you are in my heart continually, which is nothing; but it helps to persuade me that you are in the heart of Christ, which is all. — I am, dear madam, your very affectionate servant,

J. OWEN.

To Charles Fleetwood, Esq.

DEAR SIR, — I received yours and am glad to hear of your welfare. There is more then ordinary mercy in every day's preservation. My wife, I bless God, is much revived, so that I do not despair of her recovery; but for myself, I have been under the power of various distempers for fourteen days past, and do yet so continue. God is fastening his instruction concerning the approach of that season wherein I must lay down this tabernacle. I think my mind has been too much intent upon some things which I looked on as services for the church; but God will have us know that he has no need of me nor them, and is therefore calling me off from them. Help me with your prayers, that I may, through the riches of his grace in Christ, be in some measure ready for my account. The truth is, we cannot see the latter rain in its season, as we have seen the former, and a latter spring thereon. Death, that will turn in the streams of glory upon our poor withering souls, is the best relief. I begin to fear that we shall die in this wilderness; yet ought we to labour and pray continually that the heavens would drop down from above, and the skies pour down righteousness, — that the earth may open and bring forth salvation, and that righteousness may spring up together. If ever I return to you in this world, I beseech you to contend yet more earnestly than ever I have done, with God, with my own heart, with the church, to labour after spiritual revivals. Our affectionate service to your lady, and to all your family that are of the household of God. — I am, dearest sir, yours most affectionately whilst I live,

J. OWEN.

Stadham, *July* 8.

To Charles Fleetwood, Esq.

DEAR SIR, — The bearer has stayed long enough with us to save you the trouble of reading an account of me in my own scribbling: a longer stay I could not prevail with him for, though his company was a great refreshment to me. Both you and your whole family, in all their occasions and circumstances, are daily in my thoughts; and when I am enabled to pray, I make mention of you all without ceasing. I find you and I are much in complaining. For my part I must say, And is there not a cause? So much deadness, so much unspirituality, so much weakness in faith, coldness in love, instability in holy meditations, as I find in myself, is cause sufficient of complaints. But is there not cause also of thanksgiving and joy in the Lord? Are there not reasons for them? When I begin to think of them, I am overwhelmed; they are great, they are glorious, they are inexpressible. Shall I now invite you to this great duty of rejoicing more in the Lord? Pray for me, that I may do so; for the near approach of my dissolution calls for it earnestly. My heart has done with this world, even in the best and most desirable of its refreshments. If the joy of the Lord be not now strength unto it, it will fail. But I must have done. Unless God be pleased to affect some person or persons with a deep sense of our declining condition, of the temptations and dangers of the day, filling them with compassion for the souls of men, making them fervent in spirit in their work, it will go but ill with us. It may be these thoughts spring from causeless fears, it may be none amongst us has an evil, a barren heart but myself: but bear with me in this my folly; I cannot lay down these thoughts until I die; nor do I mention them at present as though I should not esteem it a great mercy to have so able a supply as Mr C., but I am groaning after deliverance; and being near the centre, do hope I feel the drawing of the love of Christ with more earnestness than formerly: but my naughty heart is backward in these compliances. My affectionate service to Sir John Hartopp, and his lady, and to the rest of your family, when God shall return them unto you. — I am, dear sir, yours most affectionately in everlasting bonds,

J. OWEN.

To the Rev. Mr Robert Asty of Norwich

DEAR SIR, — I received yours by Mr B., to whom I shall commit this return, and hope it will come safely to your hands; for although I can acknowledge nothing of what you are pleased out of your love to ascribe unto me, yet I shall be always ready to give you my thoughts in the way of brotherly advice, whenever you shall stand in need of it: and at present, as things are circumstanced, I do not see how you can waive or decline the call of the church either in conscience or reputation. For, to begin with the latter; should you do so upon the most Christian and cogent grounds in your own apprehensions, yet wrong interpretations will be put upon it; and so far as it is possible we ought to keep ourselves, not only "*extra noxam*," but "*suspicionem*" also. But the point of conscience is of more moment. All things concurring, — the providence of God in bringing you to that place, the judgment of the church on your gifts and grace for their edification and example, the joint consent of the body of the congregation in your call, with present circumstances of a singular opportunity for preaching the word, I confess at this distance I see not how you can discharge that duty you owe to Jesus Christ (whose you are, and not your own, and must rejoice to be what he will have you to be, be it more or less) in refusing a compliance unto these manifest indications of his pleasure; only, remember that you sit down and count what it will cost you, — which I know you will not be discouraged by; for the daily exercise of grace and learning of wisdom should not be grievous unto us, though some of their occasions may be irksome. For the latter part of your letter, I know no difference between a pastor and a teacher but what follows their different gifts; — the office is absolutely the same in both; the power the same, the right to the administration of all ordinances every way the same: and at that great church at Boston, in New England, the teacher was always the principal person; so was Mr Cotton and Mr Norton. Where gifts make a difference, there is a difference; otherwise there is none. I pray God guide you in this great affair; and I beg your prayers for myself in my weak, infirm condition. — I am your affectionate friend and brother,

J. Owen.
London, March 16.

To Mr Baxter

SIR, — The continuance of my cold, which yet holds me, with the severity of the weather, have hitherto hindered me from answering my purpose of coming unto you at Acton; but yet I hope, ere long, to obtain the advantage of enjoying your company there for a season. In the meantime, I return you my thanks for the communication of your papers; and shall on every occasion manifest that you have no occasion to question whether I were in earnest in what I proposed, in reference to the concord you design. For the desire of it is continually upon my heart; and to express that desire on all occasion, I esteem one part of that profession of the Gospel which I am called unto. Could I contribute any thing towards the accomplishment of so holy, so necessary a work, I should willingly spend myself and be spent in it. For what you design concerning your present essay, I like it very well, both upon the reasons you mention in your letter, as also that all those who may be willing and desirous to promote so blessed a work may have copies by them, to prepare their thoughts in reference to the whole.

For the present, upon the liberty granted in your letter (if I remember it aright), I shall tender you a few queries, which, if they are useless or needless, deal with them accordingly.

As, — 1. Are not the several proposed or insisted on too many for this first attempt? The general heads, I conceive, are not; but under them very many particulars are not only included, which is unavoidable, but expressed also which may too much dilate the original consideration of the whole.

2. You expressly exclude the Papists, who will also sure enough exclude themselves, and do, from any such agreement; but have you done the same as to the Socinians, who are numerous, and ready to include themselves upon our communion? The Creed, as expounded in the four first councils, will do it.

3. Whether some expressions suited to prevent future divisions and separations, after a concord is obtained, may not at present, to avoid all exasperation, be omitted, as seeming re-

flective on former actings, when there was no such agreement among us as is now aimed at?

4. Whether insisting in particular on the power of the magistrate, especially as under civil coercion and punishment in cases of error or heresy, be necessary in this first attempt? These generals occurred to my thoughts upon my first reading of your proposals. I will now read them again, and set down, as I pass on, such apprehensions in particular as I have of the several of them.

To the first answer, under the first question, I assent; so also to the first proposal, and the explanation; likewise to the second and third. I thought to have proceeded thus throughout, but I foresee my so doing would be tedious and useless; I shall therefore mention only what at present may seem to require second thoughts. As, —

1. To propos. 9, by those instances [what words to use in preaching, in what words to pray, in what decent habit] do you intend homilies, prescribed forms of prayer, and habits superadded to those of vulgar decent use? Present controversies will suggest an especial sense under general expressions.

2. Under pos. 13, do you think a man may not leave a church and join himself to another, unless it be for such a cause or reason as he supposes sufficient to destroy the being of the church? I meet with this now answered in your 18th propos., and so shall forbear farther particular remarks, and pass on.

In your answer to the second question, your 10th position hath in it somewhat that will admit of farther consideration, as I think. In your answer to the third question, have you sufficiently expressed the accountableness of churches mutually, in case of offence from maladministration and church censures? This also I now see in part answered, — proposition fifth. I shall forbear to add any thing as under your answer to the last question, about the power of the magistrate, because I fear that in that matter of punishing I shall somewhat dissent from you, though as to mere coercion I shall in some cases agree.

Upon the whole matter, I judge your proposals worthy of great consideration, and the most probable medium for the attaining of the end aimed at that yet I have perused. If God give not a heart and mind to desire peace and union, every expression will be disputed, under pretence of truth and accuracy; but if these things have a place in us answerable to that which they enjoy in the Gospel, I see no reason why all the true disciples of Christ might not, upon these and the like principles, condescend in love unto the practical concord and agreement, which not one of them dare deny to be their duty to aim at. Sir, I shall pray that the Lord would guide and prosper you in all studies and endeavours for the service of Christ in the world, especially in this your desire and study for the introducing of the peace and love promised amongst them that believe, and do beg your prayers. — Your truly affectionate brother, and unworthy fellow-servant,

JOHN OWEN.
Jan. 26, 1668.

III. His Works

A List of Dr Owen's Works, according to the years in which they appear to have been published.

- Display of Arminianism, 4to, 1642
- The Duty of Pastors and People Distinguished, 4to, 1643
- The Principles of the Doctrine of Christ, in two Catechisms, 12mo, 1645
- A Vision of Unchangeable Mercy: a Sermon, 4to, 1646
- Eshcol; or, Rules for Church Fellowship, 12mo, 1647
- *Salus Electorum*: a treatise on Redemption, 4to, 1648
- Memorial of the Deliverance of Essex: two Sermons, 4to, 1648
- Righteous Zeal — a Sermon; and Essay on Toleration, 4to, 1649
- The Shaking and Translating of Heaven and Earth: a sermon, 4to, 1649
- Human Power Defeated: a Sermon, 4to, 1649
- Of the Death of Christ, in answer to Baxter, 4to, 1650
- The Steadfastness of Promises: a Sermon, 4to, 1650
- The Branch of the Lord: two Sermons, 4to, 1650
- The Advantage of the Kingdom of Christ: a sermon, 4to, 1651
- The Labouring Saint's Dismission: a Sermon, 4to, 1652
- Christ's Kingdom and the Magistrate's Power: a Sermon, 4to, 1652
- *De Divina Justitia*: translated 1794, 12mo, 1653
- The Doctrine of the Saints' Perseverance, folio, 1654
- *Vindiciæ Evangelicæ*: Reply to Biddle, 4to, 1655
- On the Mortification of Sin, 8vo, 1656
- Review of the Annotations of Grotius, 4to, 1656
- God's Work in Founding Zion: a Sermon, 4to, 1656
- God's Presence with his People: a Sermon, 4to, 1656
- On Communion with God, 4to, 1657
- A Discovery of the True Nature of Schism, 12mo, 1657

- A Review of the True Nature of Schism, 12mo, 1657
- Answer to Cawdrey about Schism, 12mo, 1658
- Of the Nature and Power of Temptation, 12mo, 1658
- The Divine Original of the Scriptures, 12mo, 1659
- Vindication of the Hebrew and Greek Texts, 12mo, 1659
- *Exercitationes adversus Fanaticos*, 12mo, 1659
- The Glory of Nations professing the Gospel: a Sermon, 4to, 1659
- On the Power of the Magistrate about Religion, 4to, 1659
- A Primer for Children, 12mo, 1660
- ΘΟΛΟΓΟΥΜΕΝΑ ΠΑΝΤΟΔΑΠΑ, 4to, 1661
- Animadversions on *Fiat Lux*, 12mo, 1662
- A Discourse on Liturgies, 4to, 1662
- Vindication of the Animadversions, 8vo, 1664
- Indulgence and Toleration Considered, 4to, 1667
- A Peace-offering, or Plea for Indulgence, 4to, 1667
- Brief Instruction in the Worship of God: a Catechism, 12mo, 1667
- On Indwelling Sin, 8vo, 1668
- Exposition of the 130th Psalm, 4to, 1668
- Exposition of the Epistle to the Hebrews, vol. i., folio, 1668
- Vindication of the Doctrine of the Trinity, 12mo, 1669
- Truth and Innocence Vindicated, 8vo, 1669
- On the Divine Institution of the Lord's Day, 8vo, 1671
- On Evangelical Love, 8vo, 1672
- Vindication of the Work on Communion, 12mo, 1674
- Discourse on the Holy Spirit, folio, 1674
- Exposition of the Hebrews, vol. ii., folio, 1674
- How we may Bring our Hearts to Bear Reproof, 4to, 1674
- On the Nature of Apostasy, 8vo, 1676
- The Reason of Faith, 8vo, 1677
- On the Doctrine of Justification, 4to, 1677
- The Ways and Means of Understanding the Mind of God, 8vo, 1678
- ΧΡΙΣΤΟΛΟΓΙΑ, or the Person of Christ, 4to, 1679

- The Church of Rome no Safe Guide, 4to, 1679
- On Union among Protestants, 4to, 1680
- Vindication of the Nonconformists, 4to, 1680
- Exposition of the Hebrews, vol. iii., folio, 1680
- Defence of the Vindication, 4to, 1681
- Inquiry into Evangelical Churches, 4to, 1681
- Humble Testimony, 8vo, 1681
- On Spiritual-mindedness, 4to, 1681
- The Work of the Holy Spirit in Prayer, 4to, 1682
- The Chamber of Imagery, 4to, 1682
- An Account of the Protestant Religion, 4to, 1683
- Meditations on the Glory of Christ, part i., 8vo, 1684
- Exposition of the Hebrews, vol. iv., folio, 1684
- Of the Dominion of Sin and Grace, 8vo, 1688
- True Nature of a Gospel Church, 4to, 1689
- Meditations on the Glory of Christ, part ii., 8vo, 1691
- Two Discourses on the Work of the Spirit, 8vo, 1693
- Evidences of the Faith of God's Elect, 8vo, 1695
- Seventeen Sermons, 2 vols., 8vo, 1720
- An Answer to Two Questions; with Twelve Arguments against any Conformity to Worship not of Divine Institution, 8vo, 1720
- Sermons and Tracts, folio, 1721
- Thirteen Sermons, 8vo, 1756
- Twenty-five Discourses suitable to the Lord's Supper, 12mo, 1760

www.ingramcontent.com/pod-product-compliance
Lightning Source LLC
Chambersburg PA
CBHW011315080526
44587CB00024B/4006